ESOTERIC RELIGIOUS STUDIES SERIES

HERMETICISM AND ALCHEMY
in Renaissance Europe

1

Esoteric Religious Studies Series
HERMETICISM AND ALCHEMY
In Renaissance Europe

Author: Diohka Aesden
Publisher: Cineris Multifacet
Publication Date: 2023
ISBN: 9798397566346 (Paperback)

For inquiries and permissions, please contact:
Cineris Multifacet
cinerismultifacet@gmail.com

Design and Typesetting:
Cineris Multifacet

Cover Design:
Cineris Multifacet

Manufactured in the United States of America

First Edition: 2023

ISBN-13: 9798397566346 (Paperback)

19 54 95

CINERIS Multifacet

This page left intentionally blank.

OTHER BOOKS IN THIS SERIES

1. Hermeticism and Alchemy in Renaissance Europe
2. Gnosticism: Ancient Mystical Traditions, Sects & Texts
3. Zoroastrianism: Esoteric Teachings and the Priesthood of the Fire
4. Sufism: Persian Mystical Path of Islam
5. Daoist Immortality and Internal Alchemy
6. Theurgy and Neoplatonic Mysticism
7. Shamanism in Siberia: Animism and Nature Worship
8. African Traditional Religions and Spirituality
9. Druidism and Celtic Mysticism
10. Indigenous Australian Dreamtime, Songlines and Ancestral Beings
11. Jyotish: Vedic Astrology
12. Hellenistic Mystery Cults: Thessalian Witchcraft & Ancient Greek Magic
13. Kabbalah: Jewish Mystical Tradition
14. Shinto: Japanese Indigenous Religion
15. Native American Spirituality and Vision Quests
16. Mesoamerican Shamanism and Divination
17. Ancient Egyptian Rituals and Symbolism
18. Norse Mythology and Runes
19. Rastafarianism: Spirituality and Social Movement
20. Jainism: Ascetic Practices and Philosophy
21. Romuva: Baltic Paganism, Witchcraft, and Folklore Revival
22. Vodou: Haitian Creole Religion
23. Maori Spirituality and Creation Myths
24. Hawaiian Huna Healing and Spirituality
25. Theosophy: Blending Eastern and Western Esotericism
26. Tibetan Bon: Ancient Shamanistic Tradition
27. Yoruba Religion and Orisha Worship
28. Esoteric Buddhism: Secret Teachings and Rituals
29. Romani Folklore and Mythology
30. Aztec Mythology and Cosmology
31. Bahá'í Faith: Unity of Religions
32. Hittite Religion and Rituals
33. Spiritualism: Communication with the Spirit World
34. Afro-Caribbean Syncretic Religions
35. Tantra: Ritual Practices and Symbolism
36. Armenian Folk Religion and Beliefs
37. Guarani Mythology and Cosmology
38. Esoteric Aspects of Islam: Batiniyya and Hurufism
39. Manichaeism: Dualistic Religion and Philosophy
40. Finnish Shamanism and Folk Magic
41. Ancient Sumerian Religion and Magic
42. Afro-Brazilian Umbanda and Candomblé
43. Tibetan Oracles and Divination Practices
44. Khoisan Spirituality: San Bushmen Traditions
45. Yezidi Religion: Angel Worship and the Sacred Peacock
46. Kalash Religion: Ancient Indo-Aryan Practices
47. Druze Esotericism: Secret Wisdom and Reincarnation
48. Burmese Nat Worship and Spirit Possession
49. Ancient Canaanite Religion: Rituals, Magical Texts and Spells
50. Etruscan Divination and Augury

51. Ainu Shamanism: Spiritual Practices in Northern Japan
52. Circassian Paganism and Ancestral Customs
53. Tengrism: Central Asian Shamanistic Beliefs
54. Mari El Paganism: Volga-Finnic Indigenous Religion
55. Haida Mythology and Totemism: Healing and Spirit Communication
56. Balinese Hindu-Buddhist Syncretism
57. Aramean Religion and Ancient Semitic Cults
58. Khoekhoen Religion: Southern African Indigenous Beliefs
59. Ojibwe Midewiwin: The Grand Medicine Society
60. Afro-Colombian Religions: Palenque and Santeria
61. Sámi Shamanism: Indigenous Spirituality of Northern Europe
62. Ossetian Folk Religion and Mythology
63. Mithraism: Ancient Mystery Cult of the Roman Empire
64. Ainu Bear Festival and Symbolism
65. Ancient Anatolia: Hittites and Luwians, and Lydian Goddess Cults
66. Toda Shamanism: Indigenous People of South India
67. Mesopotamian Magic and Incantations
68. Mande Paganism: West African Traditional Religions
69. Javanese Kejawen: Mystical Teachings and Rituals
70. Thracian Myth and Greco-Roman Orphic and Dionysian Mysteries
71. Maronite Christianity: Esoteric Practices and Traditions
72. Basque Mythology, Folklore, and Witchcraft
73. Gagauz Folk Religion and Rituals
74. Tagalog Mythology: Anito Spirits and Mythical Creatures
75. Hurrian Religion: Ancient Near Eastern Pantheon
76. Buryat Buddhism: Shamanistic Elements in Tibetan Buddhism
77. Selk'nam Cosmology and Ceremonies
78. Baka Pygmy Spirituality: Central African Indigenous Beliefs
79. Kumyk Paganism: Turkic Indigenous Religion
80. Scythian Religion and Warrior Culture
81. Venda Mythology: Sacred Lake and Rainmaker Rituals
82. Onondaga Longhouse Religion: Iroquois Spiritual Practices
83. Ewe-Fon Voodoo: West African Spiritual Practices
84. Manchu Shamanism: Indigenous Spirituality of Northeast Asia
85. Taíno Religion: Indigenous Beliefs of the Caribbean
86. Ancient Moabite Religion: Worship of Chemosh and Ashtaroth
87. Gallo-Roman Religion: Celtic Influence in Roman Gaul
88. Tsimshian Mythology: Stories of Raven and Trickster Figures
89. Manobo Indigenous Spirituality: Mindanao Tribal Beliefs
90. Pawnee Sacred Bundles and Tribal Ceremonies
91. Batak Shamanism: Indigenous Practices of North Sumatra
92. Breton Folklore: Legends and Supernatural Beings
93. Jivaroan Shamanism: Indigenous Traditions of the Amazon Rainforest
94. Alawite Mystical Teachings and Secret Practices
95. Silesian Folk Religion and Folklore
96. Igbo Odinani: Traditional Religion of the Igbo People
97. Rarámuri Shamanism: Indigenous Spirituality of the Tarahumara
98. Kikuyu Traditional Religion: Sacred Sites and Ancestor Worship
99. Ancient Numidian Religion: North African Indigenous Beliefs
100. Lurs Folk Religion and Rituals

A WORLD OF ESOTERIC THOUGHT

ESOTERIC RELIGIOUS STUDIES SERIES

HERMETICISM AND ALCHEMY
in Renaissance Europe

Dedicated to

The Seven Maidens

and to

Pope Philo III

aliena familia

familiares alieni

A

ALPHA

May the reader of the Esoteric Religious Studies Series be blessed abundantly. We extend our heartfelt gratitude for your engagement with this profound exploration of esoteric traditions. As you journey through the pages, may your mind be illuminated with knowledge and your heart be filled with wisdom. May the insights and revelations within these texts expand your understanding and bring clarity to your spiritual path. May you be well-informed, enriched, and guided by the sacred wisdom that unfolds before you. May this series be a source of inspiration, transformation, and blessings upon your life.

If you enjoy the words of this book, please consider leaving a review in the marketplace you found it so that its content can reach even more interested individuals.

Table of Contents

A

Ω

INTRODUCTION

"Hermeticism and Alchemy in Renaissance Europe" dives into the fascinating world of mystical knowledge and transformative practices that flourished during the Renaissance period. This comprehensive exploration unravels the labyrinthine nexus of connections between hermeticism, a philosophical and spiritual tradition, and alchemy, the mystical art of transmutation.

In this groundbreaking work, we embark on a journey through time, traversing the elaborate atlas of Renaissance Europe, where scholars, philosophers, and alchemists sought to unlock the secrets of the universe and attain divine wisdom. Drawing from a myriad of historical sources, manuscripts, and treatises, we dive into the depths of hermetic philosophy and the multifaceted aspects of alchemical practice.

The book begins by illuminating the origins of hermeticism and alchemy, tracing their roots to ancient Egyptian, Greek, and Hellenistic traditions. We explore the pivotal role of Hermes Trismegistus, the mythical figure who embodies the fusion of Egyptian and Greek wisdom, and his legendary texts, the *Corpus Hermeticum*. These sacred texts form the cornerstone of hermetic philosophy, emphasizing the unity of all things and the pursuit of spiritual and intellectual enlightenment.

As we venture further, the book meticulously examines the seven stages of alchemy, guiding the reader through the intricate processes of *nigredo, albedo, citrinitas,* and *rubedo*. Each stage is analyzed in detail, incorporating the wisdom of renowned alchemical masters such as Ramon Llull, Paracelsus, and John Dee. We explore the symbolism, laboratory practices, and spiritual significance associated with each stage, unveiling the profound transformations sought by alchemists.

Expanding our horizons, the book reveals the hidden world of esoteric alchemy. This elusive branch of alchemy dives into the realms of secret societies, mystical rituals, and encoded knowledge. We uncover the enigmatic connection between alchemy and astrology, as celestial influences intertwine with elemental forces to shape the alchemical process.

Furthermore, the book explores the alchemical applications in the realms of medicine, art, literature, and architecture, highlighting the profound impact of alchemical thinking on various aspects of Renaissance culture. From the alchemical symbolism hidden within the works of Leonardo da Vinci to the alchemical allegories woven into dramatic plays and poetic verses, we unravel the maze-like threads that connect alchemy with the cultural atlas of Renaissance Europe.

With meticulous research and comprehensive analysis, Hermeticism and Alchemy in Renaissance Europe offers an unprecedented glimpse into the world of alchemical inquiry, shedding light on its historical context, metaphysical aspirations, and enduring influence. Join us as we embark on this intellectual and spiritual odyssey, unearthing the timeless wisdom that shaped the Renaissance and continues to allure modern minds seeking the secrets of the universe.

I: THE ORIGINS OF HERMETICISM AND ALCHEMY

The origins of Hermeticism and Alchemy trace back to the ancient civilizations of Egypt, Greece, and the Hellenistic period, where the seeds of these mystical traditions were sown. In this chapter, we dive into the early foundations of Hermeticism and Alchemy, exploring their historical context, key figures, and the intertwining of philosophical and spiritual principles.

1.1 Ancient Egypt: The Birthplace of Hermetic Wisdom

The roots of Hermeticism can be traced back to the land of ancient Egypt, a civilization known for its rich mystical and esoteric traditions. The teachings of Hermes Trismegistus, a mythical figure believed to be a fusion of the Egyptian god Thoth and the Greek god Hermes, form the core of Hermetic philosophy.

Hermes Trismegistus is credited with the authorship of the *Corpus Hermeticum,* a collection of sacred texts that expound upon the fundamental principles of the universe, the nature of divinity, and the interconnectedness of all things. These texts present a holistic worldview, blending spirituality, cosmology, and philosophical insights into a unified whole.

1.2 Greek Influence: Hermes Trismegistus and the Hellenistic Synthesis

As the Hellenistic period dawned, the wisdom of Egypt intertwined with Greek philosophical and mystical traditions, giving birth to a syncretic movement known as Hermeticism. The figure of Hermes Trismegistus emerged as the embodiment of this fusion, combining Egyptian and Greek wisdom into a unified system of knowledge.

The *Corpus Hermeticum,* believed to have been written during the early centuries of the Common Era, presents Hermes Trismegistus as a divine teacher who imparts knowledge of the spiritual and material realms. The texts expound upon topics such as the nature of the soul, theurgy (the practice of divine magic), astrology, and the pursuit of spiritual enlightenment.

1.3 Alchemy: From Egypt to Hellenistic Greece

Alchemy, closely intertwined with Hermeticism, also has its roots in ancient Egypt. The term "alchemy" is derived from the Arabic word *al-kīmiyā,* which itself traces back to the Egyptian word "khem," meaning black, referring to the fertile black soil along the Nile River.

The Egyptian alchemical tradition centered around the concept of transmutation, the transformation of base metals into noble ones, symbolizing the spiritual transformation of the alchemist. The practice of Egyptian alchemy involved the purification of metals, the creation of elixirs, and the search for the elusive *Philosopher's Stone,* believed to grant immortality and wisdom.

With the conquests of Alexander the Great, Greek culture and philosophy began to permeate Egypt, leading to a synthesis of Egyptian and Greek alchemical knowledge. This syncretism laid the foundation for the alchemical practices and ideas that would flourish during the Hellenistic and subsequent Renaissance periods.

1.4 The Renaissance Rediscovery and Revival

After centuries of obscurity, the teachings of Hermes Trismegistus and the wisdom of alchemy experienced a resurgence during the Renaissance. The rediscovery of ancient texts, including the *Corpus Hermeticum,* fueled a renewed interest in Hermeticism and alchemical pursuits.

Scholars such as Marsilio Ficino, Giovanni Pico della Mirandola, and Cornelius Agrippa played pivotal roles in translating, interpreting, and disseminating

Hermetic and alchemical knowledge. They sought to reconcile Hermetic philosophy with Christian theology, recognizing the profound spiritual and philosophical insights contained within these ancient texts.

The Renaissance period witnessed a fertile ground for the exploration of Hermeticism and alchemy, as intellectuals, alchemists, and patrons of the arts embraced the pursuit of spiritual enlightenment and the alchemical quest for transmutation.

In conclusion, the origins of Hermeticism and Alchemy can be traced back to the ancient civilizations of Egypt and Greece. The figure of Hermes Trismegistus stands as a symbol of the fusion between Egyptian and Greek wisdom, encapsulating the essence of Hermetic philosophy. The alchemical practices of ancient Egypt, with their focus on transmutation and the search for the *Philosopher's Stone,* formed the bedrock for subsequent alchemical endeavors. The Renaissance period witnessed a revival of interest in Hermeticism and alchemy, as scholars and practitioners sought to uncover the hidden wisdom contained within these mystical traditions. In the following chapters, we will dive deeper into the intricacies of alchemical processes, the symbolism, and the profound impact of these esoteric traditions on Renaissance Europe.

II: THE SEVEN STAGES OF ALCHEMY: A COMPREHENSIVE OVERVIEW

Alchemy, the mystical art of transmutation, is characterized by a profound understanding of the natural world and the pursuit of spiritual enlightenment. Central to the alchemical process are the Seven Stages, a transformative journey that the alchemist undergoes in their quest for the *Philosopher's Stone* and the attainment of higher knowledge. In this chapter, we embark on a comprehensive exploration of the Seven Stages of

Alchemy, delving into their symbolism, practices, and spiritual significance.

2.1 Nigredo: The Blackening

The first stage of alchemy, known as *Nigredo,* is represented by the color black. It is a phase of dissolution and putrefaction, where the alchemist confronts the darkness within themselves. Symbolically, this stage represents the breaking down of impurities, attachments, and false beliefs through intense self-reflection and inner work. It is a period of introspection and purification, akin to the death and decomposition of matter before new life can emerge.

2.2 Albedo: The Whitening

Following *Nigredo* comes *Albedo,* the stage of whiteness. It represents purification and the emergence of light after the darkness. Here, the alchemist continues the process of inner transformation, seeking clarity and harmony. The alchemical substances are cleansed and purified, reflecting the purification of the soul. *Albedo* signifies a state of heightened awareness and the gradual emergence of spiritual insights.

2.3 Citrinitas: The Yellowing

Citrinitas, the stage of yellowing, is marked by an intensification of spiritual illumination and the awakening of the intuitive faculties. It represents the dawn of enlightenment, where the alchemist gains deeper insights into the nature of the universe and the interconnectedness of all things. The color yellow symbolizes the radiance of the sun, signifying the alchemist's growing awareness of their place within the cosmic order.

2.4 Rubedo: The Reddening

The fourth stage, *Rubedo,* is associated with the color red, symbolizing the culmination of the alchemical process. It represents the attainment of the *Philosopher's Stone* and the union of opposites. In this stage, the alchemist experiences a profound integration of their inner selves, transcending duality and achieving spiritual wholeness. *Rubedo* signifies the alchemical wedding, a symbolic union of masculine and feminine principles, and the ultimate realization of the alchemical goal.

2.5 The Conjunctio: Union of Opposites

Within *Rubedo* lies a significant stage called the *Conjunctio,* the union of opposites. It is a pivotal moment of alchemical transformation, representing the merging of opposing elements such as *fire* and *water,* sulfur and mercury, or the sun and moon. The *Conjunctio* embodies the alchemical principle of *coincidentia oppositorum,* where the reconciliation of polarities leads to the revelation of hidden wisdom and the emergence of the divine within the self.

2.6 The Coagulatio: Solidification

The penultimate stage of alchemy is the *Coagulatio,* which signifies solidification or congealing. It represents the consolidation and integration of the alchemical work. The alchemist's newfound understanding and spiritual realization become firmly grounded, forming a stable foundation for further growth and transformation.

Coagulatio signifies the manifestation of the alchemical process in the material world.

2.7 The Sublimatio: Spiritualization

The final stage, known as the *Sublimatio,* represents the spiritualization of matter and the ascent of the soul. It is a transcendental state where the alchemist's consciousness rises above the material realm, attaining spiritual heights. The *Sublimatio* signifies the ultimate transformation of the alchemist, as they transcend their human limitations and embrace the divine essence within.

In conclusion, the Seven Stages of Alchemy provide a comprehensive framework for understanding the alchemical journey. From the initial dissolution and purification of *Nigredo* to the spiritualization and transcendence of the *Sublimatio,* these stages symbolize the transformative process that the alchemist undergoes on both a physical and metaphysical level. Each stage represents a profound shift in consciousness and an opportunity for inner growth and spiritual realization. The Seven Stages of Alchemy serve as a roadmap for the alchemist's pursuit of higher knowledge, the union of opposites, and the ultimate quest for the *Philosopher's Stone.*

III: ESOTERIC ALCHEMY: UNVEILING HIDDEN KNOWLEDGE

Alchemy, beyond its practical and material aspects, has long been associated with esoteric and mystical traditions. Esoteric Alchemy dives into the realm of hidden knowledge, unveiling the spiritual, symbolic, and metaphysical dimensions of the alchemical arts. In this chapter, we embark on a journey to explore the esoteric aspects of alchemy, revealing its hidden teachings, mystical practices, and profound insights into the nature of reality.

3.1 The Inner Work: Alchemy of the Soul

Esoteric Alchemy goes beyond the external laboratory work and dives into the inner laboratory of the soul. It recognizes that the alchemical process is not merely about transforming base metals into gold but transforming the practitioner themselves. The alchemist becomes a vessel for the transmutation of their own being, seeking to purify their thoughts, emotions, and spiritual essence.

Through rigorous self-reflection, meditation, and contemplation, the esoteric alchemist confronts their own shadow, embracing the principles of *Nigredo* and *Albedo* within their psyche. This inner work involves exploring one's unconscious patterns, fears, and limitations, ultimately leading to a state of self-realization and spiritual liberation.

3.2 The Hermetic Principles: As Above, So Below

Esoteric Alchemy draws heavily from Hermetic philosophy, which emphasizes the interconnectedness of all things. The principle of "*As above, so below*" becomes a guiding light for the esoteric alchemist. It suggests that the microcosm of the individual mirrors the macrocosm of the universe, and by understanding one's inner self, one gains insights into the workings of the cosmos.

Through the contemplation of correspondences and symbolic associations, the esoteric alchemist seeks to decipher the hidden meanings encoded in alchemical texts, symbols, and imagery. This practice of deciphering the esoteric language of alchemy unveils profound spiritual truths and reveals the interconnected nature of the physical and metaphysical realms.

3.3 The Inner Transmutation: Philosopher's Stone Within

One of the central focuses of Esoteric Alchemy is the search for the *Philosopher's Stone* within. While the external quest for the *Philosopher's Stone* involves transmuting base metals into gold, the esoteric alchemist recognizes that the true *Philosopher's Stone* is an inner realization of one's divine nature.

The *Philosopher's Stone* is seen as a metaphor for the perfected self, the integration of opposing elements, and the realization of spiritual enlightenment. The esoteric alchemist understands that the external alchemical processes mirror the inner alchemical journey of purifying, harmonizing, and transcending one's own limitations.

3.4 Rituals and Symbolism: Keys to Transformation

Esoteric Alchemy often incorporates rituals, ceremonies, and symbolic practices to facilitate spiritual transformation. These rituals serve as gateways to altered states of consciousness and the invocation of archetypal energies.

The use of symbols in esoteric alchemy holds great significance. Each symbol represents a deeper meaning and corresponds to various aspects of the alchemical process. Whether it be the serpent devouring its tail (*Ouroboros*), the *caduceus*, or the sun and moon symbols, they all hold esoteric teachings and insights into the alchemical journey.

3.5 Inner Alchemical Practices: Meditation, Visualization, and Energy Work

Esoteric Alchemy employs various inner alchemical practices to facilitate spiritual growth and transformation. Meditation, visualization, and energy work are utilized to refine and transmute the subtle energies within the practitioner.

Through meditation, the esoteric alchemist cultivates inner stillness and heightened awareness, allowing them to attune to the hidden wisdom of the alchemical process. Visualization practices enable the alchemist to work with symbolic imagery, guiding the transformation of the psyche and aligning with the energies of transmutation.

Energy work, such as working with the chakras or the circulation of subtle energies, aids in the refinement and circulation of the vital life force within the alchemist. These practices facilitate the harmonization of body, mind, and spirit, further deepening the alchemical process.

3.6 The Alchemical Quest: Integration and Unity

Esoteric Alchemy ultimately aims at the integration of the various aspects of the self and the realization of unity. The esoteric alchemist seeks to unite the masculine and feminine principles within themselves, representing the union of opposites and the balance of complementary energies.

This quest for integration extends beyond the individual and into the collective consciousness. Esoteric alchemists recognize that the transformative journey is not solely for personal gain but also contributes to the evolution and awakening of humanity as a whole.

In conclusion, Esoteric Alchemy dives into the hidden knowledge and mystical dimensions of alchemy. It explores the inner work, the contemplation of symbolism, and the practice of rituals to unveil profound insights into the nature of the self and the universe. Through the integration of opposing forces and the realization of unity, the esoteric alchemist embarks on a spiritual journey of self-transformation and enlightenment. Esoteric Alchemy serves as a guide to those seeking to unlock the hidden wisdom encoded within the alchemical arts, inviting them to explore the depths of their own being and connect with the divine essence within.

IV: PLANT ALCHEMY: THE QUEST FOR ELIXIRS AND REMEDIES

Plant Alchemy, an integral aspect of the broader alchemical tradition, focuses on the transformative powers of plants in the pursuit of elixirs and remedies. It explores the interlacing relationship between plants, their inherent properties, and their potential for healing, transformation, and spiritual growth. In this chapter, we embark on a journey through the fascinating world of Plant Alchemy, uncovering its historical context, practices, and the quest for elixirs and remedies.

4.1 The Medicinal Heritage: Ancient Roots

The use of plants for medicinal purposes dates back to ancient civilizations, where herbal remedies were employed to heal the body and restore balance. Plant Alchemy draws upon this rich heritage, incorporating the knowledge and wisdom of herbal medicine into its transformative practices.

Ancient cultures such as the Egyptians, Greeks, and Chinese recognized the healing properties of various plants and developed sophisticated systems of herbal medicine. The alchemists of the Renaissance era built upon this foundation, expanding their understanding of plants' medicinal qualities and their potential for spiritual transformation.

4.2 Spagyric Alchemy: Extracting the Quintessence

One of the key methodologies within Plant Alchemy is Spagyric Alchemy, which involves the separation, purification, and recombination of plant constituents to create potent elixirs. This process aims to extract the quintessence, or the spiritual essence, from plants.

Spagyric Alchemy utilizes various techniques such as maceration, distillation, fermentation, and calcination to extract the essential oils, volatile compounds, and mineral components from plants. By isolating and purifying these constituents, alchemists believed they could enhance their medicinal properties and unlock their spiritual potential.

4.3 Plant Spirit Communication: The Doctrine of Signatures

Plant Alchemy recognizes the interconnectedness between plants and the human psyche, incorporating the doctrine of signatures. This doctrine suggests that plants bear physical characteristics, patterns, or signatures that correspond to their medicinal or spiritual qualities.

By observing the shape, color, texture, and other features of a plant, alchemists believed they could discern its therapeutic potential. This practice of reading the signatures of plants allowed alchemists to establish a deeper connection with the plant's spirit, facilitating communication and understanding of its healing properties.

4.4 The Philosopher's Stone of Plants: Panacea and Universal Medicine

Within the realm of Plant Alchemy lies the concept of the *Philosopher's Stone* of Plants, the sought-after panacea or universal medicine. Alchemists believed that certain plants possessed extraordinary healing powers and held the potential to cure diseases, restore vitality, and prolong life.

The search for the *Philosopher's Stone* of Plants involved the identification, cultivation, and preparation of specific plant species with exceptional medicinal properties. Alchemists aimed to unlock the hidden potential of these plants, harnessing their transformative energies to create elixirs and remedies capable of restoring health and promoting spiritual growth.

4.5 Plant Alchemy and Spiritual Transformation

Plant Alchemy extends beyond physical healing and encompasses the spiritual transformation of the individual. Alchemists recognized that the properties of plants not only influenced the body but also affected the mind and spirit.

Certain plants were believed to possess psychoactive properties that could induce altered states of consciousness, visionary experiences, and spiritual insights. Alchemists utilized these plants in rituals, meditation practices, and visionary journeys to facilitate inner exploration, personal growth, and connection with the divine.

4.6 The Alchemical Garden: Cultivating Sacred Plants

Alchemists and herbalists often maintained gardens dedicated to cultivating sacred plants for alchemical purposes. These gardens were seen as sacred spaces, where the alchemical forces of nature and human intention intertwined.

In the *alchemical garden*, plants were carefully selected, grown, and nurtured to maximize their medicinal and transformative potential. The garden served as a living laboratory, providing alchemists with direct access to the raw materials necessary for their elixirs and remedies.

In conclusion, Plant Alchemy weaves together the ancient traditions of herbal medicine, alchemical processes, and spiritual exploration. It embraces the healing potential of plants, their energetic qualities, and their ability to facilitate physical, mental, and spiritual transformation. Through the practice of Spagyric Alchemy, the observation of plant signatures, and the quest for the *Philosopher's Stone* of Plants, alchemists sought to unlock the hidden powers of plants and harness their energy for the betterment of body, mind, and spirit. Plant Alchemy stands as a testament to the profound wisdom and potency of the natural world and its potential to support the alchemical journey of healing, rejuvenation, and spiritual growth..

V: METAL ALCHEMY: TRANSMUTATION AND THE PHILOSOPHER'S STONE

Metal Alchemy is a branch of alchemy that focuses on the transmutation of metals and the search for the *Philosopher's Stone*. It is a profound and detailed discipline that explores the transformative potential of metals and their connection to spiritual and metaphysical realms. In this chapter, we embark on a journey through the realm of Metal Alchemy, delving into its principles, practices, and the quest for transmutation and the *Philosopher's Stone.*

5.1 The Alchemical Transformation of Metals

Metal Alchemy centers around the belief that metals possess hidden potentials that can be unlocked through the alchemical process. Alchemists sought to transmute base metals, such as lead or mercury, into noble metals, particularly gold, as a symbolic representation of spiritual transformation and perfection.

The alchemical transformation of metals involved various techniques, including purification, separation, fusion, and distillation. These processes aimed to refine and purify the metals, removing impurities and enhancing their intrinsic properties. Alchemists believed that by working with metals and manipulating their energetic qualities, they could tap into the universal forces that govern the cosmos.

5.2 The Philosopher's Stone: The Key to Transmutation

Central to Metal Alchemy is the pursuit of the *Philosopher's Stone*, a legendary substance believed to possess the power of transmutation. The *Philosopher's Stone* was thought to have the ability to transmute base metals into gold and, on a deeper level, to catalyze the spiritual transformation of the alchemist.

The search for the *Philosopher's Stone* was a quest for hidden knowledge and spiritual enlightenment. It represented the integration of opposing forces, the unification of the material and the spiritual, and the attainment of the highest level of consciousness. Alchemists believed that the *Philosopher's Stone* held the key to understanding the nature of reality and the ultimate purpose of human existence.

5.3 Symbolism and Allegory in Metal Alchemy

Metal Alchemy employed a rich atlas of symbolism and allegory to convey its teachings and insights. The transmutation of metals was seen as a metaphor for the transformation of the human soul. Each metal corresponded to specific qualities and attributes, representing different aspects of the alchemical journey.

For example, lead symbolized the *prima materia* or the raw material of the soul, while gold represented the perfected state of spiritual realization. The stages of the alchemical process were often depicted through symbolic images, such as the phoenix rising from the ashes or the serpent devouring its tail, representing cycles of death and rebirth.

5.4 Astrology and Metal Alchemy

Astrology played a significant role in Metal Alchemy, as alchemists believed that celestial influences affected the properties and qualities of metals. The planets and their associated astrological signs were believed to impart specific energies and characteristics to metals, shaping their potential for transformation.

By understanding the planetary correspondences and astrological influences, alchemists sought to align their alchemical work with the cosmic forces, amplifying the effects of their transmutation processes. They considered astrological timing and the positioning of celestial bodies as crucial factors in conducting successful metal alchemical operations.

5.5 Practical Applications: Medicine and Metallurgy

Metal Alchemy extended beyond the realm of spiritual transformation and found practical applications in medicine and metallurgy. Alchemists believed that the transmuted metals possessed potent healing properties, capable of restoring health and vitality.

Alchemical medicines, known as "*chrysopoeia*," were created through the transmutation of metals and were believed to possess extraordinary healing abilities. These medicines were utilized to treat various ailments, purify the body, and restore balance.

In metallurgy, alchemists applied their knowledge of metal alchemy to improve the quality of metals used in various industries, such as jewelry making and coin minting. By employing alchemical techniques, they aimed to refine metals and enhance their intrinsic properties, making them more valuable and durable.

5.6 The Legacy of Metal Alchemy

Metal Alchemy has left a lasting impact on the fields of science, philosophy, and spirituality. While the literal transmutation of metals into gold remains elusive, the metaphorical and symbolic aspects of Metal Alchemy continue to encourage and influence thinkers, artists, and seekers of wisdom.

The transformative principles of Metal Alchemy transcend the physical realm, inviting individuals to embark on their own inner alchemical journey. The quest for transmutation and the *Philosopher's Stone* is a metaphor for the refinement of the self, the integration of opposing forces, and the realization of one's true nature.

In conclusion, Metal Alchemy holds a profound fascination for its exploration of the transmutation of metals and the search for the *Philosopher's Stone*. It intertwines the realms of science, spirituality, and symbolism, offering insights into the nature of transformation and the interplay between the material and the spiritual. Through the practices of purification, symbolism, and astrological alignment, Metal Alchemy invites individuals to embark on a personal alchemical journey, seeking to refine and transmute their own being in the pursuit of higher consciousness and spiritual realization.

VI: ALCHEMICAL MASTERS AND HISTORICAL FIGURES: PARACELSUS AND JOHN DEE

Alchemical Masters and historical figures played pivotal roles in the development and dissemination of alchemical knowledge. Among these influential figures, Paracelsus and John Dee hold prominent positions. In this chapter, we dive into the lives, contributions, and impact of Paracelsus and John Dee, shedding light on their alchemical pursuits, philosophical insights, and enduring legacies.

6.1 Paracelsus: The Rebel Physician and Alchemist

Paracelsus, born Philippus Aureolus Theophrastus Bombastus von Hohenheim, emerged as a revolutionary figure in the world of medicine and alchemy during the Renaissance period. Rejecting the prevailing medical theories and practices of his time, Paracelsus challenged the traditional authorities and sought to revolutionize medical treatment through his own holistic approach.

Paracelsus fused his medical knowledge with alchemical principles, emphasizing the interconnectedness of the human body, mind, and spirit. He believed that illness was not merely a physical manifestation but also a reflection of the disharmony within the individual. Through his alchemical practices, Paracelsus sought to restore balance and harmony, viewing the human body as a microcosm of the universe.

Furthermore, Paracelsus made significant contributions to pharmacology, exploring the properties and applications of various substances in his search for the "*arcana*," or hidden remedies. His approach to medicine and alchemy was deeply rooted in experimentation and observation, pioneering a more empirical and practical approach to healing.

6.2 John Dee: The Scholar, Occultist, and Advisor

John Dee, an English mathematician, astronomer, and occultist, played a multifaceted role in the world of alchemy and esoteric knowledge. He served as an advisor to Queen Elizabeth I, conducting astrological and alchemical consultations, and pursued a deep fascination with mystical and esoteric subjects.

Dee was deeply influenced by Hermeticism and sought to uncover the hidden wisdom contained within ancient texts and teachings. He believed in the existence of a universal language, which he called the "*Adamic language*," that would unveil the secrets of the universe. Dee's quest for knowledge led him to engage in multiplex occult practices, including scrying, angelic communication, and the study of angelic hierarchies.

In addition to his spiritual pursuits, Dee made significant contributions to the fields of mathematics, navigation, and astronomy. His mathematical prowess and astronomical observations aided in the advancement of scientific knowledge during his time. Dee's expansive intellect and diverse interests exemplify the interdisciplinary nature of alchemical masters.

6.3 Contributions to Alchemical Knowledge and Practices

Both Paracelsus and John Dee made substantial contributions to alchemical knowledge and practices, leaving lasting impacts on the development and understanding of alchemy.

Paracelsus emphasized the use of chemical remedies and remedies derived from minerals, plants, and animals. He introduced the concept of the "*spagyric*" method, which involved the separation, purification, and recombination of components in alchemical processes. Paracelsus's alchemical theories and practical applications paved the way for the integration of alchemy with medicine, pharmacology, and chemistry.

John Dee's contributions to alchemy lay in his exploration of symbolism, angelic communication, and mystical practices. His fascination with angelic hierarchies and the occult led to the development of complicated systems of correspondences and symbolic associations. Dee's works, such as the *Monas Hieroglyphica,* dive into the unity of all things and the interplay of symbols in alchemical transformation.

6.4 Legacy and Influence

The legacies of Paracelsus and John Dee extend far beyond their lifetimes. Their contributions to alchemical knowledge, medicine, occultism, and philosophy have had a profound and enduring influence on subsequent generations.

Paracelsus's holistic approach to medicine and his emphasis on individualized treatment laid the foundation for alternative medicine practices that continue to be explored and developed today. His integration of alchemical principles with medical practices challenged the prevailing paradigms and expanded the boundaries of healing.

John Dee's studies in symbolism, angelic communication, and occult practices paved the way for subsequent esoteric traditions and the exploration of mystical dimensions. His works continue to stimulate and enthrall scholars, occultists, and seekers of hidden knowledge.

In conclusion, Paracelsus and John Dee stand as influential figures in the realm of alchemy and esoteric knowledge. Their contributions, whether in the fields of medicine, chemistry, occultism, or philosophy, have shaped the trajectory of alchemical thought and practice. Paracelsus's holistic approach to healing and his exploration of the interconnectedness of the human body and the cosmos have left an indelible mark on medicine. John Dee's scholarly pursuits, fascination with symbolism, and occult practices have expanded the understanding of alchemy's mystical dimensions. The legacies of Paracelsus and John Dee continue to animate and guide alchemists, scholars, and seekers of wisdom on the path of transformation and spiritual realization.

VII: Metaphorical Alchemy: Inner Transformation and Spiritual Growth

Metaphorical Alchemy encompasses a realm of symbolism, imagery, and allegory that extends beyond the physical transmutation of metals. It dives into the realm of inner transformation and spiritual growth, using alchemical principles as metaphors for the journey of the soul. In this chapter, we explore the profound insights and symbolism of Metaphorical Alchemy, unraveling its hidden teachings and its potential for personal and spiritual development.

7.1 The Alchemical Journey as an Inner Quest

Metaphorical Alchemy recognizes that the alchemical process serves as a powerful metaphor for the inner journey of the individual. It mirrors the transformation of the soul, the integration of opposing forces, and the quest for spiritual enlightenment.

The various stages of alchemical transformation, such as *Nigredo, Albedo, Citrinitas,* and *Rubedo,* symbolize different aspects of the inner quest. *Nigredo* represents the confrontation with the shadow self, the darkness within, and the process of purification. *Albedo* signifies the purification of the psyche, the emergence of light, and the pursuit of clarity and wisdom. *Citrinitas* embodies the awakening of intuition and the deepening of spiritual insights. *Rubedo* represents the culmination of the inner journey, the integration of opposing forces, and the realization of unity.

7.2 The *Prima Materia*: The Raw Material of the Soul

In Metaphorical Alchemy, the concept of *prima materia,* or the raw material, takes on a symbolic meaning. It represents the unrefined, chaotic, and unmanifested aspects of the self. The *prima materia* represents the starting point of the alchemical journey, where the alchemist confronts their own imperfections, fears, and limitations.

Through the metaphorical processes of separation, purification, and recombination, the alchemist transforms the *prima materia* into a refined and integrated state. This metaphorical transmutation mirrors the individual's inner transformation, the shedding of old patterns, and the integration of their fragmented aspects.

7.3 The Philosopher's Stone as Spiritual Realization

In Metaphorical Alchemy, the *Philosopher's Stone* takes on a metaphorical significance as the ultimate goal of the spiritual journey. It represents spiritual realization, enlightenment, and the integration of the divine within the self.

The search for the *Philosopher's Stone* becomes a metaphor for the seeker's quest for self-realization and union with the divine. It symbolizes the discovery of one's true nature, the transcendent and eternal essence that lies at the core of every individual.

7.4 Symbolism and Allegory in Metaphorical Alchemy

Metaphorical Alchemy relies heavily on symbolism and allegory to convey its teachings and insights. Each stage of the alchemical process, as well as the various symbols associated with alchemy, carries profound meaning and represents different aspects of the inner journey.

For example, the symbol of the phoenix rising from the ashes embodies the cycle of death and rebirth, representing the transformative nature of the alchemical process. The serpent devouring its tail, known as the *Ouroboros*, symbolizes the eternal cycle of creation and destruction, reminding the alchemist of the need to continually shed old layers and embrace transformation.

7.5 Practical Applications: Meditation, Inner Work, and Ritual

Metaphorical Alchemy goes beyond theoretical contemplation and encourages practical applications to support inner transformation and spiritual growth. Practices such as meditation, inner work, and ritual become integral to the metaphysical alchemical journey.

Meditation serves as a tool for inner stillness, self-reflection, and the cultivation of heightened awareness. It allows the alchemist to observe their thoughts, emotions, and patterns, facilitating the process of self-realization and transformation.

Inner work involves delving into the depths of the psyche, confronting the shadow self, and integrating the fragmented aspects of the self. It requires courage, self-honesty, and a willingness to face one's fears and limitations.

Rituals provide a structured framework for the alchemical journey, enabling the alchemist to engage with symbolism, intention, and energetic practices. Rituals help to invoke and embody the archetypal energies associated with the alchemical process, facilitating a deeper connection with the transformative forces at play.

7.6 The Gift of Metaphorical Alchemy: Inner Wisdom and Self-Realization

Metaphorical Alchemy offers the gift of inner wisdom and self-realization. By engaging with the symbolic language of alchemy and the metaphorical processes of transformation, individuals gain insight into their own inner landscape and discover the path to personal and spiritual growth.

Metaphorical Alchemy teaches us that the journey of self-transformation is not limited to external achievements or material transmutations. It invites us to embark on an inner quest, embracing the challenges, and embracing the wisdom that arises from the transformative processes.

In conclusion, Metaphorical Alchemy is a profound framework for understanding and embarking on the journey of inner transformation and spiritual growth. Through symbolism, metaphor, and allegory, it guides individuals on a path of self-realization, integrating the fragmented aspects of the self, and discovering the divine essence within. Metaphorical Alchemy reminds us that the true alchemical work lies within, inviting us to embark on the transformative journey of self-discovery and spiritual awakening.

VIII: HERMES TRISMEGISTUS: THE LEGENDARY FIGURE OF ALCHEMY

Hermes Trismegistus, also known as *Thrice-Great Hermes,* is a legendary figure in the realm of alchemy and esoteric traditions. Often referred to as the "Father of Alchemy," Hermes Trismegistus embodies the fusion of Egyptian and Greek wisdom, representing the synthesis of mystical and philosophical teachings. In this chapter, we dive into the life, teachings, and enduring legacy of Hermes Trismegistus, shedding light on the profound influence this enigmatic figure has had on alchemy and spiritual traditions.

8.1 The Origin of Hermes Trismegistus

The precise origin and identity of Hermes Trismegistus remain shrouded in mystery. Hermes is associated with the Egyptian god Thoth, the god of wisdom, writing, and magic. The Greek god Hermes, known as the messenger of the gods, shares many similarities with Thoth. The merging of these two deities gave rise to the legendary figure of Hermes Trismegistus.

8.2 Hermes Trismegistus as a Teacher and Guide

Hermes Trismegistus is revered as a profound teacher and guide, offering wisdom and guidance to those on the spiritual path. His teachings encompass a vast range of subjects, including alchemy, astrology, magic, philosophy, and spirituality. Hermes is said to have authored a collection of sacred texts known as the "*Hermetica*," which explores these esoteric topics.

The *Hermetica* emphasizes the interconnection between the spiritual and material realms, encouraging individuals to seek the divine within themselves and in all aspects of existence. Hermes Trismegistus teaches that the microcosm of the individual reflects the macrocosm of the universe, and through inner transformation, one can attain a deeper understanding of the universal order.

8.3 The Principle of Correspondence and Unity

One of the key teachings of Hermes Trismegistus is the principle of correspondence, often encapsulated in the phrase "*As above, so below; as within, so without.*" This principle suggests that there is a fundamental unity and interconnection between all things in the universe. The actions and patterns observed in the celestial realm are mirrored in the earthly realm, and the inner reality of the individual is reflected in the outer world.

The principle of correspondence invites individuals to recognize the hidden patterns and interconnectedness of the universe, allowing them to access deeper insights and wisdom. By understanding the correspondence between different levels of existence, alchemists seek to uncover the hidden knowledge encoded in the symbols and processes of alchemy.

8.4 The Hermetic Philosophy and Alchemy

Hermes Trismegistus is closely associated with the development of Hermetic philosophy, which integrates mystical, philosophical, and alchemical teachings. The Hermetic tradition emphasizes the pursuit of spiritual transformation and the realization of the divine nature within oneself.

Alchemy plays a crucial role within the Hermetic tradition, as it provides a framework for the process of inner transmutation and the quest for the *Philosopher's Stone*. Hermes Trismegistus teaches that the alchemical journey is not merely about the transmutation of metals but also about the transformation of the self. Through the purification and integration of opposing forces, the alchemist seeks to attain a state of unity and spiritual realization.

8.5 Influence on Renaissance Alchemy

Hermes Trismegistus's teachings and the Hermetic tradition had a significant impact on Renaissance alchemy. During this period, scholars and practitioners sought to revive and reinterpret the wisdom contained within ancient texts, including the *Hermetica*.

The influence of Hermes Trismegistus can be seen in the works of prominent alchemists such as Paracelsus and John Dee, who drew inspiration from Hermetic philosophy and incorporated its principles into their own alchemical practices. The Hermetic tradition provided a philosophical and spiritual framework that supported the pursuit of knowledge, self-transformation, and the integration of science, spirituality, and metaphysics.

8.6 Legacy and Contemporary Significance

The teachings and legacy of Hermes Trismegistus continue to resonate with spiritual seekers, scholars, and practitioners today. His emphasis on the unity of all things, the pursuit of wisdom, and the transformative power of inner alchemy remain foundational principles in various esoteric and spiritual traditions.

The influence of Hermes Trismegistus extends beyond alchemy and has permeated diverse fields, including philosophy, religion, astrology, and magic. His teachings on the interconnectedness of the universe and the divine nature of the individual continue to uplift individuals to embark on the path of self-discovery and spiritual growth.

In conclusion, Hermes Trismegistus stands as a legendary figure in the realm of alchemy and esoteric traditions. His teachings and wisdom, encapsulated in the *Hermetica,* have shaped the development of alchemy and influenced spiritual seekers throughout history. As the guide and guardian of the alchemical journey, Hermes Trismegistus continues to energize individuals to explore the depths of their own being, discover the hidden knowledge within, and seek unity with the divine.

IX: THE VITRUVIAN MAN AND ALCHEMY: LEONARDO DA VINCI'S ALCHEMICAL INTERESTS

Leonardo da Vinci, renowned for his artistic genius and scientific inquiries, had a profound interest in alchemy. His exploration of alchemical principles and symbolism is evident in his works, including the iconic *Vitruvian Man*. In this chapter, we dive into Leonardo da Vinci's alchemical pursuits, examining the significance of the *Vitruvian Man* and uncovering the alchemical symbolism embedded within his works.

9.1 Leonardo da Vinci: The Multifaceted Genius

Leonardo da Vinci, a true Renaissance polymath, is known for his mastery in various fields, including art, engineering, anatomy, and scientific inquiry. His insatiable curiosity and keen observational skills allowed him to dive into the depths of nature, exploring the mysteries of the physical world.

Beyond his well-known artistic achievements, Leonardo da Vinci's interests extended to the esoteric realm of alchemy. His exploration of alchemy was influenced by the prevalent alchemical ideas of his time, which sought to uncover the hidden properties and transformations of matter.

9.2 The Vitruvian Man: Symbolism and Proportions

The *Vitruvian Man,* one of Leonardo da Vinci's most famous works, holds deep symbolism and significance. It depicts a male figure in two superimposed positions, with his arms and legs extended, fitting into both a *circle* and a square. This representation is based on the writings of the ancient Roman architect Vitruvius, who emphasized the importance of harmonious proportions in architecture and human anatomy.

The *Vitruvian Man* embodies the concept of the microcosm and the macrocosm, reflecting the idea that the human body is a reflection of the larger universe. The *circle* represents the celestial realm, while the square symbolizes the earthly realm. The figure's perfect proportions exemplify the harmonious relationship between humanity and the cosmos.

9.3 Alchemical Symbolism in Leonardo's Works

Leonardo da Vinci's interest in alchemy is evident in the symbolic elements and themes present in his artworks. His works often incorporate alchemical symbols, such as the sun, moon, and the *four elements* (*earth, air, fire,* and *water*). These symbols carry profound alchemical connotations, representing the transformative processes and universal forces at play.

For example, in his painting "The Last Supper," Leonardo depicts Christ holding a chalice, which is traditionally associated with the *Philosopher's Stone* in alchemy. The chalice represents the transformative elixir, capable of bestowing spiritual enlightenment and eternal life.

9.4 Transmutation and the Quest for Knowledge

Leonardo da Vinci's alchemical interests were deeply intertwined with his quest for knowledge and understanding of the natural world. Alchemists sought to transmute base metals into noble ones, reflecting the transformative power of the alchemical process.

In Leonardo's notebooks, one can find sketches and writings exploring alchemical experiments, observations on metallurgy, and the properties of various substances. His curiosity about the hidden properties of matter aligns with the alchemist's desire to uncover the secrets of transformation and the pursuit of higher knowledge.

9.5 The Integration of Science and Art

Leonardo da Vinci's alchemical pursuits exemplify his unique ability to integrate science and art. For him, the study of nature and the observation of physical phenomena went hand in hand with his artistic expression.

Through his scientific inquiries and alchemical interests, Leonardo sought to understand the underlying principles that govern the natural world. His observations of nature's intricacies influenced his artistic techniques, allowing him to depict the human form and the world around him with remarkable accuracy and depth.

9.6 The Legacy of Leonardo da Vinci's Alchemical Interests

Leonardo da Vinci's alchemical interests have left a lasting impact on the fields of art, science, and alchemy itself. His holistic approach, merging artistic expression with scientific inquiry, continues to impel and influence creators, scientists, and alchemical thinkers today.

The integration of alchemical symbolism in his works invites contemplation and exploration of the deeper layers of meaning. Leonardo's alchemical pursuits serve as a reminder of the interconnectedness between art, science, and the spiritual quest for knowledge and self-transformation.

In conclusion, Leonardo da Vinci's alchemical interests provide a glimpse into the multifaceted nature of his genius. His exploration of alchemical principles and symbolism, exemplified in the *Vitruvian Man* and other works, showcases his fascination with the transformative processes of nature. Leonardo da Vinci's alchemical pursuits serve as a testament to his unwavering curiosity, his quest for knowledge, and his belief in the interconnectedness of the physical and metaphysical realms.

X: ALCHEMICAL SYMBOLISM IN RENAISSANCE ART AND LITERATURE

The Renaissance period was marked by a resurgence of interest in alchemy, a field that blended science, spirituality, and symbolism. This era witnessed the incorporation of alchemical themes and symbols into various forms of artistic expression, including painting, sculpture, and literature. In this chapter, we explore the presence and significance of alchemical symbolism in Renaissance art and literature, highlighting its role in conveying deeper philosophical and spiritual messages.

10.1 The Marriage of Science and Art

The Renaissance was characterized by a profound shift in the way knowledge was pursued and represented. Scholars, artists, and alchemists sought to bridge the gap between science and art, viewing them as interconnected disciplines rather than separate realms.

Alchemy provided a framework for exploring the hidden mysteries of nature, and artists embraced alchemical symbolism as a means of conveying complex ideas and philosophical concepts. By incorporating alchemical symbols into their works, Renaissance artists and writers sought to tap into the transformative power of symbolism and engage with the deeper layers of meaning.

10.2 Alchemical Symbols in Visual Art

In Renaissance visual art, alchemical symbolism was often used to convey allegorical narratives or hidden spiritual teachings. Artists employed a wide range of alchemical symbols, each carrying its own significance and conveying specific ideas.

The depiction of the *Philosopher's Stone*, for example, symbolized the ultimate goal of the alchemical process and represented spiritual enlightenment and transformation. The use of serpents, dragons, and birds was common in alchemical symbolism, representing the cyclical nature of transformation, the primal forces at play, and the union of opposing elements.

Additionally, alchemical symbols such as the sun, moon, stars, and planetary bodies were incorporated into artworks to represent celestial forces and cosmic principles. These symbols emphasized the interconnectedness between the microcosm (the individual) and the macrocosm (the universe).

10.3 Alchemical Imagery in Literature

Literature of the Renaissance period also embraced alchemical symbolism as a means of conveying profound ideas and spiritual insights. Writers wove alchemical themes and imagery into their works, often employing allegory and metaphor to explore the transformative nature of the human experience.

One notable example is the work of the poet and playwright William Shakespeare. In plays like "Hamlet" and "Macbeth," Shakespeare incorporates alchemical references to explore themes of transformation, decay, and regeneration. The use of alchemical symbolism allows for a deeper exploration of the human psyche and the universal aspects of the human condition.

10.4 The Inner Alchemical Journey

Alchemical symbolism in Renaissance art and literature served as a metaphorical representation of the inner alchemical journey. It conveyed the idea that personal transformation and spiritual growth were attainable through the integration of opposing forces and the refinement of the self.

The alchemical process of purification, symbolized by the *Nigredo* stage, represented the confrontation with the shadow self and the shedding of impurities. The subsequent stages of *Albedo* (whitening), *Citrinitas* (yellowing), and *Rubedo* (reddening) were associated with the purification and refinement of the soul, leading to spiritual illumination and unity.

Through the incorporation of alchemical symbolism, Renaissance artists and writers invited audiences to embark on their own inner alchemical journey, to confront their shadow selves, and to strive for personal and spiritual transformation.

10.5 Influences of Hermeticism and Neoplatonism

The prevalence of alchemical symbolism in Renaissance art and literature was closely intertwined with the philosophical currents of Hermeticism and Neoplatonism.

Hermeticism, inspired by the teachings attributed to Hermes Trismegistus, emphasized the unity of all things and the divine nature within each individual. Neoplatonism, drawing from the philosophy of Plato, explored the interconnectedness between the physical and spiritual realms.

Both Hermeticism and Neoplatonism provided a rich source of inspiration for artists and writers, offering a framework to convey profound philosophical ideas through alchemical symbolism.

10.6 Legacy and Significance

The incorporation of alchemical symbolism in Renaissance art and literature reflects the era's fascination with the mysteries of nature, the pursuit of knowledge, and the spiritual quest for enlightenment. It highlights the Renaissance's holistic approach to understanding the world and its acknowledgment of the interconnectedness between science, art, and spirituality.

The legacy of alchemical symbolism in Renaissance art and literature continues to inspirit and enchant audiences today. It serves as a reminder that art and literature can be vehicles for profound exploration and expression, enabling individuals to dive into the depths of the human experience and contemplate the mysteries of existence.

In conclusion, alchemical symbolism played a significant role in Renaissance art and literature, offering a means of conveying complex ideas and exploring the transformative nature of the human journey. The integration of alchemical symbols provided artists and writers with a rich vocabulary to express profound philosophical and spiritual insights. The legacy of alchemical symbolism in Renaissance art and literature continues to resonate with audiences, serving as a testament to the enduring power of symbolism and the interconnectedness of human experiences.

XI: ALCHEMY AND ASTROLOGY: CELESTIAL INFLUENCES AND ELEMENTAL FORCES

Alchemy and astrology are intimately connected, as both disciplines explore the interplay between the celestial and earthly realms. Astrology recognizes the influence of celestial bodies on human lives, while alchemy dives into the transformative properties of matter and the symbolic representation of cosmic forces. In this chapter, we explore the relationship between alchemy and astrology, focusing on celestial influences and the elemental forces at play.

11.1 The Cosmic Dance: Celestial Bodies and Alchemical Principles

Astrology recognizes that celestial bodies, such as the planets and stars, exert energetic influences on human lives and the natural world. Alchemists acknowledged the correspondence between celestial energies and the principles of alchemical transformation.

Each celestial body was associated with specific qualities and attributes, reflecting the energetic influences they imparted. For example, the Sun was linked to vitality, creativity, and the masculine principle, while the Moon represented intuition, emotions, and the feminine principle. Planets like Mars, Venus, and Saturn were also assigned particular qualities and played roles in alchemical symbolism.

11.2 Elemental Forces: Earth, Air, Fire, and Water

Alchemy recognizes the importance of elemental forces in the transformative process. These forces, represented by *Earth, Air, Fire,* and *Water,* correspond to the qualities and characteristics of the elements in both astrology and alchemy.

Earth symbolizes stability, grounding, and materiality. *Air* represents intellect, communication, and the realm of ideas. *Fire* embodies passion, transformation, and the purifying aspect of the alchemical process. *Water* signifies emotions, intuition, and the fluidity of the transformative journey.

The interplay of these elemental forces is integral to both astrology and alchemy, as they shape the energetic qualities of the cosmos and the alchemical work itself.

11.3 Astrological Timing and Alchemical Operations

Astrology provides alchemists with a framework for understanding the optimal timing of alchemical operations. The positions and aspects of celestial bodies are believed to influence the success and efficacy of alchemical processes.

Alchemists would consider planetary alignments, phases of the Moon, and other astrological factors when undertaking their operations. They believed that specific celestial configurations enhanced certain aspects of the alchemical work, aligning the forces of the cosmos with their transformative intentions.

11.4 Planetary Correspondences and Alchemical Symbols

Astrology assigns specific planets to each of the seven traditional metals in alchemy. These planetary correspondences reflect the energetic qualities and transformative potentials associated with the metals.

For example, gold is linked to the Sun, representing the pinnacle of spiritual realization and the attainment of perfection. Silver corresponds to the Moon, symbolizing intuition and reflection. Mercury is associated with the planet Mercury, embodying duality and the transformation of the volatile.

These planetary correspondences serve as a bridge between astrology and alchemy, aligning the cosmic influences with the transformative processes of matter.

11.5 The Alchemical Quest for the Philosopher's Stone

The pursuit of the *Philosopher's Stone,* a legendary substance capable of transmuting base metals into gold, aligns with astrological principles. Alchemists sought to harness the cosmic energies and correspondences to unlock the transformative potential of matter and consciousness.

The *Philosopher's Stone* represented the integration of opposing forces, the union of the celestial and earthly realms, and the ultimate realization of spiritual perfection. Astrological knowledge and timing played a significant role in the alchemist's quest for the *Philosopher's Stone,* as they sought to align their work with the celestial forces that governed the alchemical process.

11.6 The Legacy of Astrological Alchemy

The connection between astrology and alchemy has left a lasting legacy, with its influence extending beyond the Renaissance period. The integration of celestial influences, elemental forces, and astrological timing continues to be explored in contemporary alchemical practices and spiritual traditions.

Astrological alchemy offers a framework for understanding the interconnectedness between the individual, the cosmos, and the transformative journey. It reminds us that we are part of a greater cosmic dance, where celestial influences and elemental forces shape our experiences and provide opportunities for growth and transformation.

In conclusion, the relationship between alchemy and astrology highlights the profound interplay between the celestial and earthly realms. Celestial bodies exert energetic influences that shape the alchemical journey, while elemental forces provide the framework for transformative processes. Astrology provides alchemists with insight into the optimal timing of operations, and planetary correspondences align cosmic forces with alchemical symbols and substances. The legacy of astrology and alchemy serves as a reminder of the deep interconnectedness of the universe and the transformative potentials that lie within the union of the celestial and the earthly.

XII: THE ALCHEMICAL LABORATORY: TOOLS, TECHNIQUES, AND PROCEDURES

The alchemical laboratory serves as the sacred space where the transformative work of alchemy takes place. It is a realm of experimentation, observation, and transformation, where alchemists engage with various tools, techniques, and procedures. In this chapter, we explore the alchemical laboratory and its essential components, shedding light on the tools used, the techniques employed, and the procedures followed in the pursuit of alchemical transformation.

12.1 The Sacred Space of the Laboratory

The alchemical laboratory is more than a physical workspace; it is a sacred space where the alchemist engages in the inner and outer work of transformation. It is a realm where the alchemist seeks to bridge the gap between the material and spiritual realms, uncovering the hidden secrets of matter and consciousness.

The laboratory is often set up with meticulous care, aligning with the alchemist's intentions and creating an environment conducive to the alchemical process. It is a place where the alchemist connects with the forces of nature, harnesses the energies of the cosmos, and embarks on the transformative journey.

12.2 Essential Tools of the Alchemical Laboratory

The alchemical laboratory is equipped with a variety of tools that aid in the practical aspects of alchemical experimentation. These tools serve as extensions of the alchemist's hands, allowing for precise measurements, mixtures, and manipulations. Some essential tools include:

1. Alembic: The alembic is a distillation apparatus used for the separation and purification of substances. It consists of a pot, a condenser, and a receiver, enabling the alchemist to extract and collect volatile components.

2. Athanor: The athanor is a slow-burning furnace used for long and controlled heating processes. It provides a consistent and steady source of heat, allowing for the slow transformation of materials.

3. Mortar and Pestle: The mortar and pestle are used for grinding, pulverizing, and blending substances. They facilitate the preparation of powders and the combining of different components.

4. Retort: The retort is a vessel with a curved neck used for distillation and sublimation processes. It allows for the collection of volatile substances while separating them from solid or impure materials.

5. Crucible: The crucible is a heat-resistant container used for high-temperature operations, such as melting metals or performing calcinations. It withstands extreme heat and allows for the transformation of substances through intense heat and purification.

6. Glassware: Various types of glassware, such as beakers, flasks, and test tubes, are used for measuring, mixing, and observing reactions. Glassware provides transparency and visibility during the alchemical processes.

These are just a few examples of the many tools used in the alchemical laboratory. Each tool has its specific purpose and contributes to the alchemist's exploration and manipulation of substances.

12.3 Techniques and Procedures in the Alchemical Laboratory

The alchemical laboratory is a space of experimentation, where alchemists employ various techniques and follow specific procedures to facilitate transformation. These techniques and procedures are based on the principles and theories of alchemy and vary depending on the specific goals and substances involved.

Some common techniques and procedures include:

1. Calcination: Calcination involves subjecting a substance to intense heat, often in a crucible, to remove impurities and initiate the process of transformation.

2. Dissolution: Dissolution is the process of dissolving a substance in a liquid, usually a solvent, to extract its essence or separate its components.

3. Coagulation: Coagulation refers to the coming together or solidification of substances, resulting in the formation of a new compound or state.

4. Fermentation: Fermentation involves the breakdown of organic matter through the action of enzymes or microorganisms, leading to the creation of new compounds or substances.

5. Distillation: Distillation is the process of separating volatile components from a substance through evaporation and subsequent condensation in a distillation apparatus, such as an alembic.

6. Sublimation: Sublimation is the transformation of a solid directly into a gas or vapor state, bypassing the liquid phase. It involves heating a substance and collecting the resulting vapor for further processing.

7. Filtration: Filtration is the process of separating solids from liquids or purifying liquids by passing them through a filter medium.

These techniques, among others, are applied in a systematic manner, following specific procedures and protocols. The alchemist's expertise, intuition, and observation skills play crucial roles in determining the appropriate techniques and procedures for each stage of the alchemical process.

12.4 The Alchemist's Mindset and Intentions

In addition to the tools, techniques, and procedures, the mindset and intentions of the alchemist are of utmost importance in the alchemical laboratory. The alchemist approaches the work with a combination of curiosity, patience, and reverence for the transformative processes at play.

The alchemist cultivates a deep understanding of the interconnectedness of all things, perceiving the inherent divinity and potential for transformation within matter. The alchemist's intentions are focused on seeking knowledge, uncovering hidden truths, and participating in the co-creative process of alchemical transformation.

By aligning their consciousness and intentions with the forces of nature and the cosmic energies, alchemists create a harmonious synergy between their inner states and the external alchemical processes.

12.5 The Spiritual Dimension of the Alchemical Laboratory

The alchemical laboratory is not merely a physical space; it is also a realm of spiritual exploration and transformation. Alchemists recognize that the outer work of manipulating substances is a reflection of the inner work of self-transformation.

The alchemical laboratory becomes a metaphorical representation of the alchemist's inner landscape, where the dross of the ego is confronted, purified, and transmuted into spiritual gold. The alchemical processes and procedures serve as metaphors for the alchemist's own journey of self-realization and spiritual evolution.

In conclusion, the alchemical laboratory is a sacred space where alchemists engage in the transformative work of alchemy. It is equipped with essential tools that aid in the practical aspects of experimentation. Techniques and procedures are employed to facilitate the transformation of substances, aligning with alchemical principles and goals. The alchemist's mindset, intentions, and spiritual understanding contribute to the alchemical process, creating a harmonious synergy between the inner and outer realms. The alchemical laboratory represents the alchemist's dedication to self-transformation, the exploration of hidden truths, and the pursuit of spiritual evolution.

XIII: Alchemical Texts and Manuscripts: Secrets of the Renaissance

The Renaissance was a time of intellectual and cultural revival, characterized by a renewed interest in the ancient wisdom and esoteric traditions. Alchemical texts and manuscripts played a significant role during this period, preserving and transmitting the secrets of alchemical knowledge. In this chapter, we explore the world of alchemical texts and manuscripts, examining their importance, the secrets they held, and their impact on the Renaissance.

13.1 The Preservation of Ancient Wisdom

Alchemical texts and manuscripts served as vessels for preserving and transmitting ancient wisdom from one generation to another. Many of these texts traced their origins to the Hellenistic and medieval periods, with influences from ancient Egypt, Greece, and the Arabic world.

During the Renaissance, scholars and alchemists sought out these ancient texts, delving into the profound teachings and symbols they contained. Alchemical manuscripts were treasured for their insights into the mysteries of nature, the transmutation of matter, and the spiritual quest for enlightenment.

13.2 The Language of Symbols and Allegory

Alchemical texts employed a unique language of symbols and allegory, making their teachings accessible to those initiated into the secrets of alchemy. Symbolism was used to convey esoteric concepts, metaphysical principles, and practical instructions in a veiled manner.

The use of symbolism allowed alchemists to encode their knowledge, protecting it from those who might misunderstand or misuse it. It also served as a means of transmitting deeper insights and spiritual teachings that could not be expressed through literal language alone.

13.3 Key Alchemical Texts of the Renaissance

Several key alchemical texts emerged during the Renaissance, becoming influential sources of alchemical knowledge. These texts encompassed a wide range of topics, including philosophical principles, practical laboratory procedures, and spiritual insights. Some notable examples include:

1. "*The Emerald Tablet*": Often attributed to Hermes Trismegistus, "*The Emerald Tablet*" is a foundational text in alchemy. It contains the famous maxim "*As above, so below*" and presents the core principles of alchemical transformation.

2. "*The Rosarium Philosophorum*": This series of illustrated alchemical treatises explores the stages of the alchemical process, using vivid imagery and allegorical narratives. It provides practical instructions and spiritual teachings for the alchemist.

3. "*The Mutus Liber*": Translated as the "Mute Book," this enigmatic work consists of a series of highly symbolic and esoteric illustrations. It is considered a visual guide to the alchemical process, conveying spiritual and transformative insights without the need for words.

4. "*The Aurora Consurgens*": This alchemical text, attributed to an anonymous author, dives into the psychological and spiritual aspects of the alchemical journey. It explores the symbolism of the union of opposites, the reconciliation of the masculine and feminine principles, and the attainment of spiritual illumination.

These texts, among many others, became foundational sources of knowledge for Renaissance alchemists, shaping their understanding of alchemical principles and providing guidance in their laboratory work and spiritual quests.

13.4 The Influence of Alchemical Manuscripts

Alchemical manuscripts had a profound impact on the Renaissance, shaping the development of alchemical thought and inspiring new avenues of inquiry. Scholars, philosophers, and artists drew upon the wisdom contained within these manuscripts, incorporating alchemical symbolism into their works.

The symbolism and teachings found in alchemical manuscripts influenced the art and literature of the Renaissance, contributing to the emergence of symbolic and allegorical traditions. The esoteric insights embedded in these manuscripts provided inspiration for painters, writers, and thinkers, fueling their creativity and expanding their understanding of the interplay between the material and spiritual realms.

13.5 The Quest for the Philosopher's Stone

One of the central themes running through alchemical texts and manuscripts of the Renaissance was the quest for the *Philosopher's Stone.* Alchemists believed that the *Philosopher's Stone* possessed the power to transmute base metals into gold, as well as to bestow spiritual enlightenment and immortality.

Alchemical texts often discussed the properties, preparation, and symbolism of the *Philosopher's Stone,* presenting it as the ultimate goal of the alchemical process. These texts offered clues, allegorical narratives, and practical instructions to aid the alchemist on their quest for this elusive and transformative substance.

13.6 The Legacy of Alchemical Texts

The alchemical texts and manuscripts of the Renaissance continue to mystify and rouse researchers, scholars, and enthusiasts today. Their encoded wisdom and rich symbolism invite exploration and contemplation, offering insights into the interconnectedness of the physical and spiritual realms.

These texts serve as a reminder of the quest for knowledge, the pursuit of transformation, and the eternal longing for the secrets of the universe. They illuminate the intellectual and spiritual currents that shaped the Renaissance, leaving a lasting legacy in the fields of alchemy, art, philosophy, and esoteric traditions.

In conclusion, alchemical texts and manuscripts were vital repositories of ancient wisdom during the Renaissance. They preserved and transmitted the secrets of alchemical knowledge, using symbolism and allegory to convey esoteric teachings. These texts shaped the understanding of alchemical principles, influenced the art and literature of the period, and inspired the pursuit of transformation and enlightenment. The legacy of these texts continues to fascinate and exhilarate seekers of wisdom and truth in the modern world.

XIV: THE CHYMICAL WEDDING OF CHRISTIAN ROSENKREUTZ: A ROSICRUCIAN ALCHEMICAL ALLEGORY

"*The Chymical Wedding of Christian Rosenkreutz*" is a significant alchemical allegory that emerged during the Renaissance period. It is considered a foundational text of the Rosicrucian movement, a mystical and philosophical tradition that sought to integrate spiritual and scientific knowledge. In this chapter, we explore "*The Chymical Wedding of Christian Rosenkreutz*," examining its symbolism, themes, and its significance as a Rosicrucian alchemical allegory.

14.1 The Origins of the Text

"*The Chymical Wedding of Christian Rosenkreutz*" was first published in 1616, anonymously and under the guise of an ancient text. It describes the spiritual journey of Christian Rosenkreutz, the fictional protagonist, through a series of seven days. The text gained attention and became associated with the Rosicrucian movement, a secret society that claimed to possess esoteric knowledge and sought to reform society through the integration of science, spirituality, and alchemy.

14.2 Symbolism and Allegory

"*The Chymical Wedding of Christian Rosenkreutz*" is rich in symbolism and allegory, inviting readers to explore deeper levels of meaning. The text serves as a metaphorical representation of the alchemical process and the spiritual journey of the seeker.

Christian Rosenkreutz's journey through seven days is reminiscent of the stages of alchemical transformation. Each day represents a different stage of the alchemical process, starting with the *Nigredo* (blackening) and progressing through stages such as *Albedo* (whitening), *Citrinitas* (yellowing), and *Rubedo* (reddening). These stages correspond to the purification and refinement of the alchemist's consciousness and soul.

14.3 The Themes Explored

"*The Chymical Wedding of Christian Rosenkreutz*" explores several key themes that are central to the Rosicrucian tradition and alchemy as a whole. These themes include:

1. Spiritual Transformation: The text emphasizes the transformative journey of the seeker, both in the alchemical and spiritual sense. Christian Rosenkreutz undergoes a series of trials and experiences that lead to his inner transformation and spiritual enlightenment.

2. Union of Opposites: The alchemical concept of the union of opposites is central to the text. The characters and situations encountered by Christian Rosenkreutz represent the merging and reconciliation of opposing forces, such as the masculine and feminine, the spiritual and material, and the divine and earthly.

3. Integration of Science and Spirituality: The Rosicrucian movement sought to bridge the gap between scientific knowledge and spiritual wisdom. "*The Chymical Wedding of Christian Rosenkreutz*" reflects this integration, as the text weaves alchemical symbolism, scientific concepts, and spiritual insights together, emphasizing the unity of these seemingly disparate realms.

4. Divine Love and the Mystic Marriage: The text explores the theme of divine love and the mystical union of the soul with the divine. Christian Rosenkreutz's journey culminates in a symbolic marriage ceremony, representing the union of the seeker's soul with the divine essence and the attainment of spiritual wholeness.

14.4 The Impact and Significance

"*The Chymical Wedding of Christian Rosenkreutz*" had a profound impact on the development of the Rosicrucian movement and subsequent esoteric traditions. The text captured the imagination of readers, inspiring them to embark on their own inner alchemical and spiritual journeys.

The allegorical nature of the text allowed for multiple interpretations and engaged readers on intellectual, spiritual, and symbolic levels. It served as a catalyst for deeper exploration and contemplation of alchemical principles, spiritual transformation, and the integration of diverse knowledge systems.

"*The Chymical Wedding of Christian Rosenkreutz*" also contributed to the dissemination of alchemical ideas and influenced subsequent alchemical texts and manuscripts. Its themes and symbolism resonated with other alchemical traditions, leaving a lasting legacy in the field of esoteric and mystical literature.

In conclusion, "*The Chymical Wedding of Christian Rosenkreutz*" stands as a significant Rosicrucian alchemical allegory. Through its symbolism and themes, the text invites readers to contemplate the transformative journey of the seeker, the integration of scientific and spiritual knowledge, and the mystical union of the soul with the divine. Its impact on the Rosicrucian movement and the broader alchemical tradition cannot be overstated, as it inspires and entrances seekers of wisdom and truth to this day.

XV: THE ALCHEMICAL SOCIETY OF RENAISSANCE EUROPE

During the Renaissance, the pursuit of alchemical knowledge and spiritual transformation sparked the formation of various alchemical societies and organizations throughout Europe. These societies provided a platform for alchemists to exchange ideas, conduct experiments, and explore the depths of alchemical wisdom. In this chapter, we dive into the world of the Alchemical Society of Renaissance Europe, examining its origins, activities, key figures, and its role in the advancement of alchemical knowledge.

15.1 The Emergence of Alchemical Societies

The Renaissance was a period of intellectual and cultural awakening, characterized by a thirst for knowledge and a desire to unlock the secrets of the universe. Alchemy, with its blend of science, spirituality, and symbolic language, captured the minds of scholars, philosophers, and seekers of wisdom. As a result, alchemical societies began to emerge, serving as focal points for the exchange of ideas and the advancement of alchemical knowledge.

15.2 The Purpose and Activities of the Alchemical Society

The Alchemical Society of Renaissance Europe was founded with the aim of fostering collaboration, sharing discoveries, and supporting the research and practice of alchemy. The society provided a platform for alchemists to present their findings, engage in discussions, and refine their understanding of alchemical principles and processes.

Activities within the society included the presentation of research papers, the demonstration of laboratory techniques, and the sharing of experimental results. Alchemists would often engage in debates, challenging one another's theories and interpretations, with the ultimate goal of advancing the collective understanding of alchemy.

15.3 Key Figures of the Alchemical Society

The Alchemical Society of Renaissance Europe attracted prominent figures in the field of alchemy, drawing together some of the most renowned alchemists of the time. These individuals made significant contributions to the society's activities and played a pivotal role in the advancement of alchemical knowledge.

One such figure was Paracelsus, a Swiss alchemist and physician known for his innovative ideas and unorthodox approaches to medicine and alchemy. Paracelsus's participation in the society provided a platform for him to present his revolutionary theories and challenge the prevailing beliefs of his time.

Another notable member of the society was John Dee, an English mathematician, astrologer, and alchemist. Dee's contributions to the society included his insights into astrology, mathematics, and symbolic interpretation, which greatly influenced the alchemical discourse of the time.

These and other prominent figures of the Alchemical Society of Renaissance Europe brought their unique perspectives, experimental findings, and philosophical insights to the table, enriching the discussions and pushing the boundaries of alchemical understanding.

15.4 Research and Experimentation

The Alchemical Society of Renaissance Europe was a hub for research and experimentation. Alchemists would conduct experiments in their laboratories, seeking to uncover the secrets of transmutation, the purification of matter, and the spiritual transformation of the self.

Experimental findings and observations were presented and discussed within the society, allowing for the refinement of techniques and the development of new theoretical frameworks. The society served as a catalyst for innovation and discovery, pushing alchemists to push the boundaries of their knowledge and challenge established beliefs.

15.5 The Exchange of Ideas and Knowledge

One of the key functions of the Alchemical Society of Renaissance Europe was the exchange of ideas and knowledge among its members. Alchemists from different regions would gather to share their insights, experiences, and discoveries, creating a rich atlas of diverse perspectives.

Through the exchange of ideas, alchemists would refine their understanding of alchemical principles, learn from one another's experiments, and build upon each other's findings. The society became a fertile ground for the cross-pollination of ideas, leading to new discoveries and the evolution of alchemical thought.

15.6 The Legacy of the Alchemical Society

The Alchemical Society of Renaissance Europe left a lasting legacy in the field of alchemy and contributed to the advancement of scientific and philosophical thought during the Renaissance. The society provided a framework for collaboration, research, and experimentation, fostering the growth of alchemical knowledge and pushing the boundaries of human understanding.

The exchange of ideas and knowledge within the society contributed to the dissemination of alchemical principles, influencing subsequent generations of alchemists, philosophers, and scientists. The legacy of the society can be seen in the continued exploration of alchemy and its influence on fields such as chemistry, psychology, and esoteric traditions.

In conclusion, the Alchemical Society of Renaissance Europe played a vital role in the advancement of alchemical knowledge during the Renaissance. It provided a platform for the exchange of ideas, the sharing of experimental findings, and the refinement of alchemical techniques and theories. The society attracted key figures in the field and served as a catalyst for innovation and discovery. Its legacy continues to resonate in the fields of science, philosophy, and esoteric traditions, emphasizing the enduring influence of alchemy on human understanding.

XVI: ALCHEMY AND MEDICINE: HEALING THE BODY AND SOUL

Alchemy and medicine have long been intertwined, as both disciplines share a common goal: the healing and transformation of the human body and soul. Throughout history, alchemists have explored the enmeshed connections between the physical and spiritual realms, seeking to unlock the secrets of health, longevity, and spiritual well-being. In this chapter, we dive into the relationship between alchemy and medicine, examining how alchemical principles and practices have influenced the field of healing.

16.1 The Alchemical Paradigm of Healing

Alchemy views the human body as a microcosm of the universe, with its own energetic and spiritual dynamics. It recognizes that the health of the body is intricately linked to the state of the soul and the balance of energies within. Alchemists sought to restore harmony and balance through their understanding of the principles of transformation and purification.

The alchemical paradigm of healing goes beyond mere physical remedies; it encompasses the holistic approach of addressing the root causes of illness and disharmony. Alchemists recognized that physical symptoms often had underlying psychological, emotional, or spiritual origins. By addressing these deeper aspects, they believed true healing could be achieved.

16.2 The Doctrine of Signatures

One of the key concepts in alchemical medicine is the doctrine of signatures. This doctrine suggests that nature provides signs and symbols that indicate the medicinal properties of various plants, minerals, and substances. Alchemists believed that these signatures were encoded by a divine intelligence, allowing humans to decipher the healing potential of different substances.

For example, a plant with a yellow flower was thought to have properties that could benefit the liver or the digestive system. A substance resembling the human organ it was intended to heal was believed to possess restorative powers. The doctrine of signatures guided alchemists in the identification and application of healing substances.

16.3 Spagyric Medicine

Spagyric medicine is a branch of alchemy that focuses on the extraction, purification, and recombination of the active constituents of plants and minerals. The term "*spagyric*" comes from the Greek words "*spao*" (to separate) and "*ageiro*" (to combine). Alchemists used specific techniques to separate the various components of a plant or mineral, purify them, and then recombine them to create potent medicines.

The goal of *spagyric* medicine was to capture the essential life force or spirit of the plant or mineral, which was believed to possess powerful healing properties. By employing alchemical processes, such as distillation, fermentation, and calcination, alchemists aimed to enhance the therapeutic qualities of medicinal substances and make them more bioavailable for the body.

16.4 Alchemical Symbolism in Medicine

Alchemical symbolism played a significant role in the practice of medicine. Alchemists used symbols and allegorical language to represent the qualities and properties of different substances and their effects on the body and soul. These symbols conveyed not only the physical attributes of the substance but also their energetic and spiritual qualities.

For example, the symbol of the serpent shedding its skin was associated with renewal and rejuvenation, indicating the potential of a substance to restore vitality and promote healing. The sun, with its association with light and warmth, symbolized life force and energy.

By understanding the symbolic language of alchemy, physicians could prescribe treatments and remedies that aligned with the specific needs of the individual, taking into account their physical, emotional, and spiritual well-being.

16.5 Spiritual Alchemy and Inner Healing

Alchemy recognizes that true healing goes beyond the physical body; it encompasses the healing of the soul and the transformation of consciousness. Spiritual alchemy seeks to transmute the base aspects of the human psyche into higher virtues and qualities, leading to spiritual awakening and inner illumination.

The alchemical processes of purification, transformation, and transmutation parallel the stages of spiritual growth and self-realization. As alchemists sought to refine and purify matter, they also sought to refine and purify the soul, freeing it from the constraints of ego and facilitating its connection with the divine.

By incorporating spiritual alchemy into the practice of medicine, healers can address not only the symptoms of illness but also the underlying spiritual imbalances that contribute to disease. This holistic approach recognizes that true healing involves the integration of body, mind, and spirit.

16.6 The Legacy of Alchemy in Medicine

The influence of alchemy on medicine can be seen throughout history and continues to resonate in modern healing practices. Many concepts and techniques rooted in alchemical principles have found their way into contemporary medicine and complementary healing modalities.

The emphasis on holistic healing, the recognition of the mind-body connection, and the integration of spiritual and energetic aspects of health can all be traced back to alchemical teachings. The alchemical paradigm of healing reminds us that true health involves more than the absence of disease; it encompasses the harmonious interplay of physical, emotional, and spiritual well-being.

In conclusion, the relationship between alchemy and medicine is profound and multifaceted. Alchemy's holistic approach to healing, its use of symbolism and the doctrine of signatures, the practice of *spagyric* medicine, and its emphasis on spiritual alchemy all contribute to a comprehensive understanding of health and well-being. The legacy of alchemy in medicine reminds us that true healing involves the integration of body, mind, and spirit, leading to transformation, harmony, and the realization of our highest potential.

XVII: ALCHEMICAL ALLEGORIES IN RENAISSANCE DRAMA AND POETRY

The Renaissance period witnessed a flourishing of artistic expression, including dramatic plays and poetry that were deeply influenced by the alchemical tradition. Alchemical allegories became a popular and powerful tool for exploring spiritual, philosophical, and psychological themes in literature. In this chapter, we explore the presence and significance of alchemical allegories in Renaissance drama and poetry, examining their symbolism, themes, and their contribution to the literary landscape of the time.

17.1 The Symbolic Language of Alchemy

Alchemy, with its rich symbolism and metaphoric language, provided fertile ground for the development of allegorical representations in literature. Alchemists used symbols and allegories to convey deeper meanings and hidden truths, allowing for multiple layers of interpretation. This symbolic language found its way into Renaissance drama and poetry, creating a dynamic interplay between the literal and the metaphorical.

17.2 Alchemical Themes in Renaissance Drama

Renaissance playwrights drew upon alchemical symbolism and concepts to explore a range of themes in their dramatic works. These themes included transformation, the search for spiritual enlightenment, the reconciliation of opposites, and the journey of self-discovery.

For example, in William Shakespeare's play "The Tempest," alchemical motifs are woven throughout the narrative. The character of Prospero, the magician and alchemist, represents the transformative power of the human spirit. Through his art and wisdom, he orchestrates a series of events that lead to redemption and reconciliation.

In Christopher Marlowe's play "Doctor Faustus," the titular character's pursuit of forbidden knowledge can be seen as an alchemical quest for enlightenment and power. The play explores the consequences of Faustus's choices and his eventual spiritual downfall, mirroring the alchemical notion of the dangers of imbalanced pursuits.

17.3 Alchemical Imagery in Renaissance Poetry

Renaissance poets also embraced alchemical imagery and allegory as a means of exploring complex themes and expressing profound insights. Poetic works of the time often utilized alchemical symbols and metaphors to convey hidden truths and to evoke deeper emotions in the reader.

The poetry of John Donne, for instance, frequently employs alchemical imagery and language. In his poem "*A Valediction: Forbidding Mourning,*" Donne uses the metaphor of the compass to describe the connection between two souls in love, symbolizing the alchemical union of opposites.

The metaphysical poets, including George Herbert and Andrew Marvell, also incorporated alchemical symbolism into their works. Their poems explored themes of spiritual transformation, the divine marriage of the soul, and the pursuit of transcendent experiences.

17.4 Psychological and Philosophical Insights

Alchemical allegories in Renaissance drama and poetry were not merely decorative devices; they offered profound psychological and philosophical insights. The exploration of alchemical themes allowed playwrights and poets to dive into the complexities of the human psyche, the nature of existence, and the quest for self-realization.

By using alchemical symbolism, authors could dive into the transformative processes of the human psyche, representing the journey of individuation and the integration of the shadow and the anima/animus aspects of the self. The alchemical stages of purification, separation, conjunction, and transmutation provided a framework for exploring the psychological growth and development of characters.

17.5 The Legacy of Alchemical Allegories

The use of alchemical allegories in Renaissance drama and poetry left a lasting impact on the literary landscape. These allegories expanded the horizons of artistic expression, blending spiritual and philosophical concepts with imaginative storytelling. They invited audiences and readers to contemplate deeper meanings and truths, fostering a sense of wonder and introspection.

The legacy of alchemical allegories can be seen in the continued exploration of symbolism, metaphor, and psychological depth in literature. They influenced subsequent generations of writers, poets, and playwrights, inspiring them to incorporate symbolic elements and metaphorical language to convey complex ideas and emotions.

In conclusion, alchemical allegories enriched Renaissance drama and poetry, providing a platform for exploring spiritual, psychological, and philosophical themes. The symbolic language of alchemy allowed playwrights and poets to dive into the depths of human experience, inviting audiences to contemplate the transformative power of the soul and the search for higher truths. The legacy of alchemical allegories continues to resonate in literature, reminding us of the enduring power of symbolism and metaphor in capturing the complexities of the human condition.

XVIII: THE ALCHEMICAL INFLUENCE ON RENAISSANCE SCIENCE AND PHILOSOPHY

The Renaissance period marked a significant shift in scientific and philosophical thought, with alchemy playing a pivotal role in shaping these fields. Alchemical principles, practices, and symbolism influenced the development of scientific inquiry and philosophical discourse during this time. In this chapter, we explore the alchemical influence on Renaissance science and philosophy, examining how alchemy contributed to the advancement of knowledge and the transformation of intellectual paradigms.

18.1 Alchemy as a Precursor to Modern Science

Alchemy laid the groundwork for modern scientific inquiry by emphasizing empirical observation, experimentation, and the systematic pursuit of knowledge. Alchemists sought to understand the hidden workings of nature, exploring the properties and transformations of matter through laboratory experiments. Their practical approach to understanding the physical world paved the way for the emergence of the scientific method.

18.2 Transmutation and the Search for Knowledge

One of the central pursuits of alchemy was the transmutation of base metals into noble metals, particularly the transformation of lead into gold. While the literal transmutation remained elusive, alchemists recognized the metaphorical and philosophical implications of this quest.

The pursuit of transmutation represented a quest for knowledge, a striving to uncover the secrets of nature and the cosmos. Alchemists believed that by mastering the art of transmutation, they could gain insight into the underlying principles governing the universe. This search for knowledge became a driving force in both scientific and philosophical endeavors of the Renaissance.

18.3 Symbolism and Allegory in Science and Philosophy

Alchemy employed a rich language of symbolism and allegory to convey its teachings. This symbolic language influenced scientific and philosophical discourse, allowing for the exploration of abstract concepts and complex ideas.

For example, the alchemical concept of the "*Philosopher's Stone*" served as a metaphor for the ultimate goal of knowledge and enlightenment. It represented the synthesis of opposing forces, the union of the material and spiritual realms, and the attainment of higher wisdom. This symbolic representation influenced Renaissance thinkers, encouraging them to seek profound insights and understanding through their intellectual pursuits.

18.4 Paracelsian Medicine and the Holistic Approach

Paracelsus, a renowned Renaissance alchemist and physician, revolutionized medical theory and practice. His approach to medicine, known as Paracelsian medicine, integrated alchemical principles and holistic healing methods. Paracelsus emphasized the interconnectedness of the body, mind, and spirit, viewing health and disease as manifestations of imbalances within this triad.

Paracelsian medicine emphasized the use of herbal remedies, alchemical preparations, and energetic therapies to restore harmony and balance in the body. This holistic approach, rooted in alchemical principles, contributed to the development of modern integrative medicine and influenced subsequent medical practices.

18.5 Hermeticism and the Unity of All Things

Hermeticism, an esoteric tradition rooted in ancient Egypt and influenced by alchemical principles, had a profound impact on Renaissance thought. Hermetic philosophy emphasized the interconnectedness of all things, the unity of the microcosm and the macrocosm.

Hermetic principles permeated scientific and philosophical discussions, inspiring thinkers to explore the harmonious relationships between the natural world, the human psyche, and the divine. This holistic perspective influenced the development of systems thinking and the understanding of the interconnectedness of all aspects of existence.

18.6 Alchemy and the Transformation of Consciousness

Alchemy went beyond the physical transformation of matter; it sought the transformation of consciousness and the evolution of the human spirit. Alchemical practices aimed to purify the soul, elevate consciousness, and facilitate spiritual growth.

This focus on inner transformation had a profound impact on Renaissance philosophy, particularly in the development of philosophical systems such as Neoplatonism and Hermetic philosophy. These systems emphasized the pursuit of wisdom, self-realization, and the union of the individual soul with the divine.

18.7 The Legacy of Alchemical Influence

The alchemical influence on Renaissance science and philosophy left a lasting legacy. The alchemical emphasis on experimentation, observation, and the pursuit of knowledge laid the foundation for the scientific method. Alchemical symbolism and metaphorical language enriched philosophical discourse, inviting deeper contemplation and exploration of abstract concepts.

Furthermore, the holistic and integrative approach of alchemy in fields such as medicine and psychology continues to influence contemporary practices. The recognition of the interconnectedness of body, mind, and spirit has shaped modern approaches to health and well-being.

In conclusion, the alchemical influence on Renaissance science and philosophy was profound and far-reaching. Alchemy's practical methodologies, symbolic language, and philosophical teachings contributed to the development of scientific inquiry, holistic healing practices, and profound philosophical systems. The legacy of this influence continues to shape our understanding of the world and our place within it, reminding us of the enduring power of alchemical wisdom and its impact on the Renaissance and beyond.

XIX: ALCHEMY AND THE COURT: PATRONAGE AND INFLUENCE

Alchemy, with its blend of science, philosophy, and spiritual wisdom, captured the imagination of many rulers and nobles during the Renaissance period. The courts of kings and queens became centers of alchemical patronage, where alchemists were supported, encouraged, and provided with the necessary resources to pursue their research and experiments. In this chapter, we explore the relationship between alchemy and the court, examining the patronage and influence that shaped the practice and development of alchemy during the Renaissance.

19.1 The Fascination of the Nobility

The pursuit of alchemy by the nobility was fueled by several factors. Firstly, alchemy was seen as a means of acquiring great wealth through the transmutation of base metals into gold. The allure of this potential wealth and the power it represented was a significant draw for many rulers.

Secondly, alchemy was believed to hold the key to prolonging life, achieving immortality, and accessing hidden wisdom. The nobility sought these benefits for themselves, viewing alchemy as a means to transcend human limitations and attain higher states of being.

Lastly, alchemy offered the promise of esoteric knowledge and secrets that could enhance the prestige and influence of rulers. The possession of alchemical wisdom was seen as a symbol of power and enlightenment, which further motivated the nobility to support and engage with alchemists.

19.2 Patronage of Alchemists

Renaissance courts provided a supportive environment for alchemists, offering financial resources, access to laboratories, and protection from potential persecution. Rulers recognized the potential benefits of alchemical discoveries and sought to harness them for their own purposes.

Prominent alchemists, such as Paracelsus and John Dee, found patrons within the courtly circles. Paracelsus received support from various rulers, including the Duke of Württemberg and the Prince of Anhalt. His innovative ideas and medical insights were valued, leading to his appointment as court physician and the establishment of alchemical laboratories.

John Dee, an English mathematician, astronomer, and alchemist, found patronage from Queen Elizabeth I. Dee's knowledge and skills in astrology and alchemy made him a valued advisor to the queen, who sought his insights on matters of state.

19.3 Alchemy and Courtly Symbolism

The association between alchemy and the court extended beyond financial patronage. Alchemical symbolism and ideas found their way into courtly rituals, ceremonies, and the symbolism of royal power. Alchemical motifs, such as the sun, moon, and various alchemical stages, were incorporated into courtly art, architecture, and heraldry, conveying messages of power, wisdom, and divine right.

The adoption of alchemical symbolism allowed rulers to align themselves with the transformative powers and esoteric knowledge associated with alchemy. It served to enhance their legitimacy, elevate their status, and establish a connection between their rule and the divine order of the cosmos.

19.4 Alchemy and Diplomacy

Alchemy also played a role in diplomatic relations between courts. Rulers would exchange alchemical knowledge, experiments, and findings as a form of intellectual and cultural exchange. Alchemical manuscripts, treatises, and laboratory techniques were shared, often as diplomatic gifts, fostering cooperation and communication between rulers.

The exchange of alchemical knowledge allowed rulers to demonstrate their intellectual prowess, their support for scientific and philosophical inquiry, and their commitment to seeking wisdom and enlightenment. It also served as a means of establishing alliances and fostering mutual understanding between different courts.

19.5 The Influence of Courtly Patronage

The patronage of alchemy by the nobility had a profound influence on the practice and development of alchemy during the Renaissance. The financial support provided by rulers allowed alchemists to conduct experiments, procure materials, and establish laboratories. This support fostered innovation and advancement in alchemical techniques and theories.

Additionally, the patronage of the nobility elevated the status of alchemists and conferred credibility to their work. Alchemists were able to collaborate with scholars, philosophers, and other practitioners, leading to the exchange of ideas and the cross-pollination of knowledge. The patronage of the courts created a vibrant intellectual environment where alchemists thrived and contributed to the broader intellectual and scientific landscape of the time.

19.6 The Legacy of Alchemical Patronage

The patronage of alchemy by the courts left a lasting legacy. It supported the preservation and dissemination of alchemical knowledge, allowing it to transcend generations and influence subsequent scientific and philosophical movements. The courtly patronage of alchemy also contributed to the integration of scientific inquiry, philosophical exploration, and spiritual wisdom, setting the stage for the emergence of modern science and the development of human knowledge.

In conclusion, the patronage of alchemy by the courts during the Renaissance played a crucial role in the practice and development of alchemy. The nobility's fascination with alchemy, motivated by the pursuit of wealth, immortality, and esoteric wisdom, led to financial support and protection for alchemists. Alchemy became intertwined with courtly symbolism, diplomacy, and cultural exchange, shaping the intellectual and cultural landscape of the time. The legacy of courtly patronage continues to influence our understanding of alchemy, the interplay of science and power, and the enduring quest for knowledge and transformation.

XX: THE ROLE OF WOMEN IN RENAISSANCE ALCHEMY

The Renaissance period was marked by a significant contribution of women to various fields, including art, literature, and science. While women faced numerous societal challenges and restrictions, some managed to break through these barriers and make notable advancements in the field of alchemy. In this chapter, we explore the role of women in Renaissance alchemy, highlighting their contributions, challenges, and the lasting impact they had on the development of alchemical knowledge.

20.1 Women Alchemists: An Unveiling of Hidden Figures

Throughout history, the contributions of women in alchemy have often been overlooked or overshadowed by their male counterparts. However, recent research has revealed the significant presence of women alchemists during the Renaissance period. These women were scholars, practitioners, and experimenters who actively engaged in the pursuit of alchemical knowledge.

20.2 The Challenges Faced by Women Alchemists

Women alchemists faced numerous challenges and barriers that hindered their full participation in the field. Social norms, gender biases, and limited educational opportunities were significant hurdles for women seeking to engage in scholarly pursuits. Access to alchemical resources, such as laboratories and texts, was often restricted or denied to women.

Despite these obstacles, some women alchemists managed to overcome societal constraints and make significant contributions. Their determination, intelligence, and resilience allowed them to navigate a predominantly male-dominated field.

20.3 Notable Women Alchemists

Several women made noteworthy contributions to Renaissance alchemy. Among them was Cleopatra the Alchemist, who lived during the third century and was renowned for her alchemical experiments and writings. Her works on alchemical processes and the preparation of medicinal substances influenced subsequent generations of alchemists.

Another notable figure was Mary the Jewess, an Alexandrian alchemist from the second century. Mary is credited with pioneering various alchemical techniques and apparatus, such as the water bath and the alembic. Her writings, though few have survived, provided valuable insights into the practical aspects of alchemy.

20.4 Caterina Sforza: A Renaissance Alchemical Patron

While not an alchemist herself, Caterina Sforza, an influential Italian noblewoman of the Renaissance, played a crucial role in supporting and promoting alchemy. Caterina served as a patron to numerous alchemists, providing financial resources, materials, and protection.

Her patronage facilitated the work of alchemists such as Giovanni Ambrogio Lanfranchi, who conducted experiments and research under her support. Caterina's contribution as a patron highlights the important role played by women in enabling and encouraging alchemical endeavors during the Renaissance.

20.5 Women's Influence on Alchemical Knowledge

Women alchemists brought their unique perspectives and insights to the field, contributing to the expansion and diversification of alchemical knowledge. Their contributions encompassed various aspects of alchemy, including experimentation, theoretical writings, and practical applications.

Women alchemists often focused on the medicinal and pharmaceutical aspects of alchemy, exploring the preparation of remedies and elixirs. Their expertise in herbalism and medicinal plants brought valuable insights into the healing properties of natural substances.

20.6 The Legacy of Women in Renaissance Alchemy

The contributions of women alchemists during the Renaissance left a lasting legacy on the development of alchemical knowledge. Their work challenged prevailing gender norms, opened doors for future generations of women, and demonstrated the potential for women to excel in scientific and scholarly pursuits.

The achievements of women alchemists paved the way for increased recognition of women's contributions to the broader field of science. They served as inspiration for later generations of women scientists and alchemists, reminding us of the importance of diverse perspectives and the need to empower women in scientific exploration.

In conclusion, women played a significant but often overlooked role in Renaissance alchemy. Despite facing numerous challenges, women alchemists made important contributions to the field, advancing alchemical knowledge and expanding the understanding of the transformative powers of nature. Their achievements serve as a testament to the resilience, intellect, and determination of women in the pursuit of scientific and alchemical endeavors.

XXI: THE MAGNUM OPUS: ACHIEVING THE GREAT WORK IN ALCHEMY

The *Magnum Opus*, meaning the Great Work, is the ultimate goal of alchemy. It represents the pursuit of inner transformation, the transmutation of base matter into spiritual gold, and the attainment of enlightenment. In this chapter, we dive into the concept of the *Magnum Opus*, exploring its symbolism, stages, and the profound implications it holds within the realm of alchemy.

21.1 The Philosophical Journey

The *Magnum Opus* is not merely a physical or chemical process but a profound philosophical and spiritual journey. It represents the alchemist's quest for self-realization, the understanding of the universe, and the connection between the microcosm (the individual) and the macrocosm (the cosmos).

21.2 Symbolism and Stages

The *Magnum Opus* is often depicted through a series of symbolic stages, each representing a particular phase of the alchemical process. While the exact symbolism and terminology may differ among alchemists, some common stages are widely recognized:

1. *Nigredo* (Blackening): The initial stage represents the dissolution and decomposition of the *prima materia,* the base material. It symbolizes the breaking down of the ego, confronting one's shadows, and facing the darkness within.

2. *Albedo* (Whitening): The second stage involves purification and the removal of impurities. It represents the cleansing of the soul, the awakening of spiritual insight, and the attainment of inner clarity.

3. *Citrinitas* (Yellowing): The third stage signifies the emergence of the soul's inner light. It represents the development of wisdom, the integration of opposites, and the harmonization of conflicting elements within the self.

4. *Rubedo* (Reddening): The final stage represents the culmination of the Great Work. It symbolizes the union of opposites, the integration of body and spirit, and the attainment of spiritual gold. It signifies the alchemical transformation of the individual, resulting in a state of enlightenment and transcendence.

21.3 Inner and Outer Alchemy

The *Magnum Opus* encompasses both inner and outer alchemy. While outer alchemy focuses on the transformation of physical matter, inner alchemy pertains to the transformation of the individual's consciousness and spirit. The two are deeply interconnected, as the outer processes mirror the inner journey of the alchemist.

21.4 The Union of Opposites

Central to the concept of the *Magnum Opus* is the union of opposites. Alchemists seek to reconcile and integrate opposing forces within themselves, such as the masculine and feminine, the conscious and unconscious, and the physical and spiritual. This union represents the attainment of wholeness, balance, and harmony.

21.5 The *Prima Materia*

The *prima materia*, meaning the primary material, is a fundamental concept in alchemy. It represents the raw, formless substance from which all creation arises.

The alchemical process involves the transformation and refinement of the *prima materia,* leading to the manifestation of its true essence.

21.6 The Spiritual Quest

The *Magnum Opus* is ultimately a spiritual quest, a journey of self-discovery and self-transcendence. It represents the alchemist's yearning for spiritual awakening, liberation from the limitations of the ego, and communion with the divine.

21.7 Philosophical Implications

The concept of the *Magnum Opus* holds profound philosophical implications. It challenges the notion of separation between matter and spirit, highlighting the interconnectedness of all things. It emphasizes the transformative potential of the human spirit and the pursuit of higher states of consciousness.

Furthermore, the *Magnum Opus* encourages self-reflection, introspection, and personal growth. It invites individuals to confront their inner shadows, transcend their limitations, and embrace the journey of self-realization.

In conclusion, the *Magnum Opus* represents the pinnacle of the alchemical journey, the pursuit of self-transformation, and the attainment of spiritual enlightenment. It encompasses the reconciliation of opposing forces, the purification of the soul, and the union of the individual with the cosmos. The concept of the *Magnum Opus* carries profound philosophical and spiritual implications, inspiring individuals to embark on their own inner alchemical journey, seeking the realization of their highest potential.

XXII: ALCHEMY AND HERMETIC PHILOSOPHY: THE QUEST FOR UNIVERSAL KNOWLEDGE

Alchemy and Hermetic philosophy share a deep connection, both in terms of their origins and their underlying principles. Hermeticism, rooted in ancient Egypt and attributed to the mythical figure Hermes Trismegistus, encompasses a wide range of esoteric teachings and mystical traditions. In this chapter, we explore the relationship between alchemy and Hermetic philosophy, highlighting their shared quest for universal knowledge and their profound impact on spiritual, philosophical, and scientific thought.

22.1 The Hermetic Tradition

The Hermetic tradition emerged from ancient Egypt and was later influenced by Greek philosophy. At the heart of Hermetic teachings is the pursuit of wisdom, enlightenment, and the understanding of the universe's inner workings. The writings attributed to Hermes Trismegistus, collectively known as the *Hermetica*, formed the core texts of this tradition.

22.2 The Seven Hermetic Principles

Hermetic philosophy is characterized by its emphasis on certain fundamental principles that govern the nature of reality. These principles provide insights into the workings of the universe and guide the seeker of wisdom. Among the most renowned principles are:

1. *The Principle of Mentalism*: This principle asserts that the universe is fundamentally mental, with the mind as the

underlying fabric of all existence. It suggests that our thoughts and consciousness shape our reality.

2. *The Principle of Correspondence*: This principle posits that there is a correspondence between the macrocosm (the universe) and the microcosm (the individual). It suggests that the patterns and laws observed in the larger universe can be found within ourselves.

3. *The Principle of Vibration*: According to this principle, everything in the universe is in a state of constant vibration. All matter, energy, and consciousness are characterized by varying frequencies and vibrational patterns.

4. *The Principle of Polarity*: This principle highlights the presence of opposites and dualities in the universe. It suggests that these opposing forces are necessary for growth, balance, and the manifestation of higher states of consciousness.

5. *The Principle of Rhythm*: This principle recognizes the existence of cycles and rhythms in the universe. It suggests that everything experiences periods of expansion and contraction, ebb and flow, and that these rhythms can be harnessed and aligned with for personal growth.

6. *The Principle of Cause and Effect*: This principle asserts that every action has a corresponding reaction. It emphasizes personal responsibility and the notion that individuals are co-creators of their reality.

7. *The Principle of Gender*: This principle acknowledges the presence of masculine and feminine energies in all things. It suggests that these energies, when harmonized and balanced, contribute to the creation and transformation of the universe.

22.3 Alchemy and the Hermetic Tradition

Alchemy and Hermetic philosophy share common origins and core principles. Both traditions seek the transformation and purification of the self, the understanding of the hidden laws of nature, and the attainment of higher wisdom. Alchemy, in many ways, can be seen as an applied form of Hermetic philosophy, employing practical techniques to explore and manifest the universal principles.

The symbolism and practices of alchemy align with the Hermetic teachings. Alchemists viewed the transmutation of base metals into gold as a metaphorical process of spiritual transformation, mirroring the alchemist's journey of purifying the soul and attaining enlightenment. The alchemical laboratory became a microcosm reflecting the macrocosmic principles of the universe.

22.4 The Influence of Hermeticism on Renaissance Thought

Hermetic philosophy had a profound impact on Renaissance thought, shaping scientific, philosophical, and religious discourse. The revival of ancient texts attributed to Hermes Trismegistus sparked a renewed interest in esoteric knowledge and spiritual practices.

Hermetic ideas influenced thinkers such as Marsilio Ficino, Giovanni Pico della Mirandola, and Giordano Bruno, who sought to reconcile Hermetic teachings with Christian theology. These philosophers integrated Hermetic concepts into their philosophical systems, exploring the relationship between the divine, the human, and the natural world.

22.5 The Legacy of Hermeticism and Alchemy

The Hermetic tradition and alchemy continue to resonate in contemporary spiritual and philosophical thought. Their emphasis on the quest for wisdom, the interconnectedness of all things, and the potential for personal transformation inspires individuals to embark on their own inner journeys of self-discovery.

Hermetic principles, such as mentalism, correspondence, and cause and effect, are reflected in modern metaphysical and New Age teachings. The legacy of Hermeticism and alchemy can be seen in the integration of spiritual, scientific, and philosophical perspectives, fostering a holistic understanding of the universe and our place within it.

In conclusion, alchemy and Hermetic philosophy are intimately intertwined, sharing a quest for universal knowledge, wisdom, and self-transformation. The Hermetic principles of mentalism, correspondence, and polarity find expression in alchemical symbolism and practices. The influence of Hermeticism on Renaissance thought and its continued impact on contemporary spiritual and philosophical discourse highlight the enduring significance of these traditions.

XXIII: ALCHEMICAL TRANSMISSIONS: INFLUENCES FROM THE EAST AND ISLAMIC WORLD

Alchemy, as a rich and diverse tradition, has been influenced by various cultures and regions throughout history. The transmission of alchemical knowledge and practices extended beyond Europe, encompassing the East and the Islamic world. In this chapter, we explore the influences from the East and the Islamic world on alchemy, examining the cross-cultural exchange, the blending of ideas, and the contributions that enriched the alchemical tradition.

23.1 Transmission of Knowledge along the Silk Road

The Silk Road, an ancient network of trade routes connecting the East and the West, served as a conduit for the transmission of knowledge and ideas, including alchemy. As goods, technologies, and philosophies traversed this vast network, alchemical teachings also made their way across borders, allowing for the exchange and fusion of diverse perspectives.

23.2 Chinese Alchemy: Daoist Influences

Chinese alchemy, rooted in Daoist philosophy, played a significant role in shaping alchemical traditions. Daoism emphasized harmony with nature, the cultivation of inner energy (*qi*), and the pursuit of immortality. Chinese alchemists developed comprehensive systems of inner alchemy, focusing on the refinement and transmutation of the self.

The concept of the elixir of life, a substance believed to grant immortality, featured prominently in Chinese alchemical practices. Chinese alchemy also emphasized the balance between yin and yang energies, the transformation of the five elements (*wood, fire, earth, metal,* and *water*), and the use of medicinal herbs and minerals.

23.3 Indian Alchemy: Rasayana and the Quest for Transformation

Indian alchemy, known as *Rasayana,* emerged from the Vedic traditions and influenced the alchemical landscape. *Rasayana* sought not only the transmutation of metals but also the transformation of the individual. It incorporated practices such as yoga, meditation, and the use of alchemical elixirs to promote longevity, rejuvenation, and spiritual evolution.

The Indian alchemical tradition placed great importance on the balance and refinement of the three *doshas* (*vata, pitta,* and *kapha*) and the integration of the physical, mental, and spiritual aspects of the self. It also explored the concept of the alchemical elixir as a catalyst for inner transformation and the attainment of higher states of consciousness.

23.4 Islamic Alchemy: The Golden Age of Knowledge

During the Islamic Golden Age, from the 8th to the 14th centuries, alchemy flourished in the Islamic world. Scholars translated and synthesized Greek, Persian, and Indian alchemical texts, preserving and expanding upon the knowledge inherited from these traditions.

Islamic alchemists made significant contributions to various fields, including chemistry, medicine, and metallurgy. They developed sophisticated laboratory techniques, refined distillation methods, and expanded the understanding of chemical processes. Islamic alchemy also embraced spiritual and metaphysical aspects, exploring the symbolic and esoteric dimensions of alchemical transformation.

23.5 The Influence of Eastern and Islamic Alchemy on European Alchemy

The transmission of alchemical knowledge from the East and the Islamic world to Europe had a profound impact on European alchemy. The integration of Eastern and Islamic ideas expanded the scope of European alchemical practice, enriching its philosophical and practical dimensions.

Eastern and Islamic concepts, such as the balance of opposing forces, the refinement of the self, and the pursuit of spiritual enlightenment, influenced European alchemists. The symbolism and allegorical language of Eastern and Islamic alchemical traditions found resonance within European texts, fostering the development of new perspectives and insights.

23.6 The Legacy of Eastern and Islamic Alchemy

The influences from the East and the Islamic world left a lasting legacy on the alchemical tradition. The integration of Eastern and Islamic perspectives expanded the understanding of alchemy, highlighting its holistic nature and emphasizing the interconnectedness of the physical, mental, and spiritual realms.

Furthermore, the transmission of alchemical knowledge fostered cross-cultural exchange and intellectual dialogue. It contributed to the flourishing of scientific, philosophical, and artistic endeavors, leaving a lasting impact on the broader cultural landscape of the regions involved.

In conclusion, alchemy benefitted greatly from the cross-cultural transmissions and influences from the East and the Islamic world. Chinese, Indian, and Islamic alchemical traditions provided unique perspectives, practices, and insights that enriched the broader alchemical tradition. The legacy of these influences keeps inspiring contemporary seekers of wisdom, emphasizing the interconnectedness of diverse cultural traditions and the universal quest for transformation and enlightenment.

XXIV: THE ALCHEMICAL LEGACY: IMPACT AND SIGNIFICANCE IN MODERN TIMES

Alchemy, with its rich history and profound teachings, continues to have a significant impact in modern times. While its traditional practices may have evolved or transformed, the fundamental principles and philosophical underpinnings of alchemy continue to resonate in various fields of study and aspects of human life. In this chapter, we explore the enduring legacy of alchemy, examining its impact and significance in the modern world.

24.1 Psychological and Spiritual Growth

One of the enduring legacies of alchemy is its emphasis on psychological and spiritual growth. Alchemical symbolism and practices provide a framework for understanding the transformative journey of the self. Concepts such as the union of opposites, the purification of the soul, and the attainment of enlightenment encourages individuals on their paths of personal development and self-discovery.

Psychological approaches, such as Jungian psychology, have drawn heavily from alchemical principles. Carl Jung recognized the symbolism and *archetypes* present in alchemical texts and used them as a means to explore the depths of the human psyche. The concept of individuation, the process of becoming one's true self, bears strong parallels to the alchemical quest for self-realization.

24.2 Scientific Inquiry and Discovery

Alchemy played a pivotal role in the development of early scientific inquiry. While the alchemical practices of transmutation and the search for the *Philosopher's Stone* may not have yielded the literal transformation of base metals into gold, they laid the groundwork for modern chemistry.

The experimental methods, laboratory techniques, and observations employed by alchemists contributed to the emergence of empirical science. Alchemy's emphasis on observation, experimentation, and the systematic pursuit of knowledge set the stage for the development of the scientific method, which remains foundational to scientific inquiry today.

24.3 Symbolism and Artistic Expression

Alchemy's rich symbolism and allegorical language maintains its inspiration on artistic expression. The painstakingly coded imagery and metaphors found in alchemical texts and illustrations have been a source of inspiration for painters, writers, musicians, and film-makers.

Artists have drawn upon alchemical symbolism to explore themes of transformation, personal growth, and the interplay of opposites. The use of alchemical motifs in literature, visual arts, and music provides a means of expressing complex ideas and inviting contemplation.

24.4 Integrative Medicine and Holistic Healing

Alchemy's holistic approach to healing, which integrates the physical, mental, and spiritual dimensions of the individual, has influenced modern approaches to healthcare. The principles of balance, harmony, and the interconnectedness of all aspects of existence continue to resonate in the field of integrative medicine.

Integrative medicine combines conventional medical treatments with complementary and alternative therapies, recognizing the importance of addressing the whole person. Alchemical concepts, such as the balance of opposing forces and the use of natural remedies, have influenced practices such as herbal medicine, energy healing, and mind-body therapies.

24.5 Personal Transformation and Self-Development

The alchemical legacy has found resonance in the realm of personal transformation and self-development. The metaphorical language of alchemy and its teachings on the transmutation of the self offer valuable insights into the process of inner growth and self-actualization.

Various self-help and personal development approaches draw upon alchemical principles, encouraging individuals to embrace the transformative journey, confront their shadows, and integrate opposing aspects of themselves. The alchemical metaphor of the *Philosopher's Stone* as a symbol of personal wholeness and enlightenment still inspires individuals on their paths of self-discovery.

24.6 The Quest for Wisdom and Meaning

Alchemy's enduring legacy lies in its invitation to seek wisdom and meaning in life. The alchemical pursuit of universal knowledge, the understanding of hidden truths, and the exploration of the mysteries of existence insists on inspiring individuals in their quest for purpose and fulfillment.

In a world where knowledge is increasingly specialized and compartmentalized, alchemy reminds us of the interconnectedness of all things and invites us to embrace a holistic approach to understanding ourselves and the world around us.

In conclusion, the alchemical legacy persists in the modern world, impacting various domains of human inquiry and experience. Whether in the realms of psychology, science, art, healing, or personal development, alchemy's principles of transformation, balance, and interconnectedness continue to resonate. The enduring significance of alchemy lies in its invitation to embrace the journey of self-discovery, pursue wisdom, and cultivate a deeper understanding of the mysteries of existence.

XXV: ALCHEMICAL SYMBOLS AND THEIR MEANINGS

Alchemy, with its rich symbolism and allegorical language, utilized a vast array of symbols to convey its teachings and insights. These symbols, often steeped in mysticism and metaphor, carry profound meanings and offer a visual representation of the alchemical processes and principles. In this chapter, we explore some of the key alchemical symbols and their meanings, shedding light on the hidden wisdom they hold.

25.1 The Ouroboros

The *Ouroboros* is a powerful symbol representing cyclicality, infinity, and the eternal nature of existence. It depicts a serpent or dragon biting its own tail, forming a continuous *circle*. The *Ouroboros* signifies the perpetual cycle of creation and destruction, the interdependence of opposites, and the process of transformation.

Within alchemy, the *Ouroboros* embodies the idea of the alchemical cycle, where the *prima materia* undergoes a series of transformations, eventually returning to its original state. It symbolizes the alchemist's journey of self-realization, the dissolution of the ego, and the union of opposites.

25.2 The Philosopher's Stone

The *Philosopher's Stone* is one of the most renowned symbols in alchemy. It represents the ultimate goal of the alchemical process: the transmutation of base metals into gold and the attainment of spiritual enlightenment. The *Philosopher's Stone* is depicted as a radiant, luminous substance, often represented as a red or white stone.

Symbolically, the *Philosopher's Stone* signifies the alchemist's inner transformation and the integration of opposing forces within the self. It represents the embodiment of spiritual perfection, the attainment of wisdom, and the harmonization of body, mind, and spirit.

25.3 The Caduceus

The *Caduceus* is a symbol associated with Hermes, the Greek god of alchemy and communication. It consists of a staff or rod, entwined by two serpents, with wings at the top. The *Caduceus* is a representation of balance, harmony, and the union of opposing forces.

In alchemy, the *Caduceus* symbolizes the reconciliation and integration of dualities, such as the masculine and feminine energies. It represents the alchemist's quest for wholeness, the awakening of higher consciousness, and the alignment of the individual with the cosmic order.

25.4 The Sun and Moon

The Sun and Moon are central symbols in alchemy, representing opposing but complementary forces. The Sun is associated with masculine energy, light, and active principles, while the Moon represents feminine energy, darkness, and passive principles.

The Sun and Moon symbolize the union of opposites and the alchemical process of conjunction, where opposing elements merge to create a new entity. They also represent the interplay between conscious and unconscious aspects of the self, the integration of reason and intuition, and the pursuit of balance and harmony.

25.5 The Four Elements

The *Four Elements—Earth, Air, Fire,* and *Water—* are fundamental symbols in alchemy, representing the building blocks of all matter and the forces of nature. Each element is associated with specific qualities and properties.

Earth symbolizes stability, grounding, and the material realm. *Air* represents intellect, communication, and the realm of ideas. *Fire* signifies transformation, passion, and the energy of change. *Water* embodies emotions, intuition, and the realm of the subconscious.

In alchemy, the *Four Elements* signify the alchemist's understanding of the interconnectedness of all things and the need to balance these elemental forces within the self for spiritual growth and harmony.

25.6 The Hexagram

The Hexagram, also known as the Star of David or Solomon's Seal, is a six-pointed star formed by two overlapping triangles. It is a symbol of unity, balance, and the integration of opposing forces.

In alchemy, the Hexagram represents the union of *fire* and *water*, the masculine and feminine energies, and the spiritual and material realms. It signifies the alchemist's pursuit of the Middle Path, the harmonization of dualities, and the attainment of equilibrium.

25.7 The Cross and the Crucible

The Cross and the Crucible are symbols associated with the process of purification and transformation in alchemy. The Cross represents the intersection of the material and the spiritual, while the Crucible symbolizes the vessel in which the alchemical processes take place.

Together, the Cross and the Crucible signify the alchemist's willingness to undergo the trials and challenges of the transformative journey. They represent the crucifixion of the ego, the surrender of the self to the alchemical processes, and the eventual resurrection and renewal.

25.8 The Triangle and the Square

The Triangle and the Square are geometric symbols frequently used in alchemical texts and illustrations. The Triangle, with its three sides, represents the trinity, the triune nature of existence, and the interplay of opposing forces. The Square signifies stability, foundation, and the material realm.

The Triangle and the Square symbolize the alchemical concept of the quaternio, the union of opposites. They represent the integration of spiritual and material aspects, the fusion of transcendent and immanent qualities, and the alchemist's pursuit of balance and unity.

25.9 The Green Lion and the Red Lion

The Green Lion and the Red Lion are alchemical symbols associated with the processes of dissolution and coagulation. The Green Lion represents the initial stage of dissolution, where the alchemist breaks down the *prima materia,* representing the chaotic and formless aspects of the self. The Red Lion signifies the subsequent stage of coagulation, where the purified essence is solidified and transformed into a higher state.

These symbols signify the alchemist's journey of self-deconstruction and reconstruction, the dissolution of the ego, and the transformation of the individual into a higher state of being.

25.10 The Feathered Serpent

The Feathered Serpent is a symbol found in various cultures and traditions, including alchemy. It combines the attributes of the serpent, representing transformation and wisdom, with the ethereal qualities of feathers, symbolizing lightness, transcendence, and spiritual ascent.

The Feathered Serpent signifies the alchemist's ascent from the earthly realm to the spiritual realm, the shedding of limitations, and the attainment of higher consciousness.

In conclusion, alchemical symbols carry deep meanings and provide visual representations of the philosophical and transformative principles of alchemy. The *Ouroboros*, the *Philosopher's Stone*, the *Caduceus*, the Sun and Moon, the *Four Elements*, the Hexagram, the Cross and Crucible, the Triangle and Square, the Green Lion and Red Lion, and the Feathered Serpent are just a few examples of the symbols used in alchemy. These symbols offer insights into the nature of existence, the processes of transformation, and the quest for wisdom and self-realization. They continually inspire contemplation and serve as reminders of the profound wisdom embedded in the alchemical tradition.

XXVI: THE ALCHEMICAL IMAGINATION: ARCHETYPES AND SYMBOLISM

The realm of alchemy, with its meticulous symbolism and allegorical language, taps into the depths of the human psyche and sparks the imagination. Alchemical texts and illustrations are replete with *archetypes* and symbols that resonate with universal themes and awaken the alchemical imagination within us. In this chapter, we dive into the world of *archetypes* and symbolism in alchemy, exploring their psychological and transformative significance.

26.1 Archetypes: Patterns of the Collective Unconscious

Archetypes, as conceptualized by Carl Jung, are universal, primordial patterns or images that reside in the collective unconscious. They represent the fundamental structures of human experience and possess a transcultural and transhistorical quality. In alchemy, *archetypes* play a central role, appearing in symbolic forms that evoke deep-seated emotions, instincts, and insights.

26.2 The Self: The Archetype of Wholeness

The *Self* is a central *archetype* in alchemy, representing the totality of the psyche and the integration of all opposing elements. It embodies the unity of conscious and unconscious, masculine and feminine, and spiritual and material aspects of the self. The journey toward the realization of the *Self* lies at the heart of the alchemical quest for transformation and self-actualization.

26.3 The Shadow: Confronting the Unconscious

The *Shadow archetype* represents the repressed and disowned aspects of the self, the hidden and often darker parts of our personality. In alchemy, the confrontation and integration of the *Shadow* are vital for psychological wholeness. The alchemical process involves delving into the depths of the unconscious, acknowledging and integrating the *Shadow*, and reclaiming lost parts of the self.

26.4 The Anima and Animus: Balancing Opposing Energies

The *Anima* and *Animus archetypes* embody the feminine and masculine energies, respectively, within individuals of both genders. They represent the unconscious counterpart of one's gender and play a significant role in inner balance and psychological integration. Alchemy emphasizes the exploration and integration of these opposing energies, leading to the harmonization of the individual's psyche.

26.5 The Wise Old Man and the Wise Old Woman

The Wise Old Man and the Wise Old Woman *archetypes* symbolize wisdom, guidance, and the embodiment of accumulated knowledge and experience. They represent the inner wisdom and guidance that emerges through the alchemical journey. These *archetypes* often appear as mentors, guides, or alchemical masters in the alchemist's quest for transformation.

26.6 The Alchemical Wedding: Union of Opposites

The concept of the *Alchemical Wedding* embodies the union of opposites, the integration of masculine and feminine energies, and the realization of wholeness. It signifies the inner alchemical process where the individual merges with the divine, leading to spiritual enlightenment and transformation. The *Alchemical Wedding* represents the culmination of the alchemist's journey and the realization of the *Self*.

26.7 The Great Mother and the Divine Child

The Great Mother *archetype* symbolizes nurturing, fertility, and the creative force of nature. It represents the source of life, the embodiment of the feminine principle, and the transformative power of creation. The

Divine Child *archetype* represents rebirth, innocence, and the potential for new beginnings. Together, they signify the cyclical nature of life and the transformative power of the creative process.

26.8 Symbolism: Language of the Unconscious

Symbolism in alchemy serves as a bridge between the conscious and unconscious realms, allowing for the expression of complex ideas, emotions, and spiritual insights. Alchemical symbols, such as the *Ouroboros,* the *Philosopher's Stone,* the *Caduceus,* and the *Four Elements,* carry deep meanings and speak to the depths of the human psyche. They evoke imagery and emotions that resonate with the archetypal realm and spark the alchemical imagination.

26.9 The Transformative Power of Archetypes and Symbolism

The *archetypes* and symbolism in alchemy hold transformative power. They evoke deep-seated emotions, insights, and intuitions, inviting individuals to embark on their own inner alchemical journey. Engaging with alchemical *archetypes* and symbols allows for self-reflection, the exploration of unconscious aspects, and the integration of opposing forces. The transformative potential lies in the realization of wholeness, the reconciliation of dualities, and the expansion of consciousness.

26.10 The Alchemical Imagination: Personal and Collective Transformation

The alchemical imagination, fueled by *archetypes* and symbolism, serves as a catalyst for personal and collective transformation. It opens doors to new perspectives, initiates psychological growth, and offers a framework for understanding the profound mysteries of existence. The alchemical journey, guided by the archetypal realm and enriched by symbolism, unlocks the potential for self-discovery, self-realization, and the expansion of consciousness.

In conclusion, the alchemical imagination is nourished by *archetypes* and symbolism, serving as a gateway to psychological and spiritual transformation.

The archetypal patterns of the *Self*, the *Shadow*, the *Anima* and *Animus*, the *Wise Old Man and Woman*, the *Alchemical Wedding*, the *Great Mother and Divine Child*, among others, offer profound insights into the human psyche. Alchemical symbolism, serving as the language of the unconscious, evokes deep meaning and stirs the alchemical imagination within us. Engaging with these *archetypes* and symbols opens the path to personal and collective transformation, inviting us to explore the depths of our being and embrace the fullness of our potential.

XXVII: ALCHEMY IN RENAISSANCE MUSIC: HARMONIES OF TRANSFORMATION

The Renaissance period was a time of great intellectual and artistic flourishing, characterized by the revival of ancient knowledge and the exploration of new ideas. Alchemy, with its profound symbolism and transformative principles, influenced various disciplines, including music. In this chapter, we dive into the world of alchemy in Renaissance music, exploring the harmonies of transformation and the interplay between alchemical concepts and musical expression.

27.1 Music as an Alchemical Language

Music, like alchemy, is a language that transcends words, evoking emotions, and speaking to the depths of the human experience. It has the power to touch the soul, transform moods, and transport listeners to other realms. In the Renaissance period, composers and musicians sought to embody the transformative principles of alchemy within their compositions, utilizing musical structures, harmonies, and symbolic motifs.

27.2 The Quest for Harmony and Balance

Alchemy emphasizes the reconciliation and integration of opposing forces, and this concept finds resonance in the musical realm. Renaissance composers explored the interplay of contrasting musical elements, such as consonance and dissonance, light and dark tonalities, and tension and release. Through their compositions, they sought to create harmonies that reflect the alchemical quest for balance and unity.

27.3 Musical Symbolism and Allegory

Just as alchemical texts employ symbolism and allegory to convey their teachings, Renaissance composers utilized musical symbolism to convey deeper meanings. Musical motifs and themes were associated with specific concepts or emotions, allowing for layers of interpretation and evoking alchemical imagery.

For example, the motif of rising and falling melodic lines could represent the ascent and descent of consciousness, mirroring the alchemical journey. The use of specific intervals or chord progressions might evoke the symbolism of the *Philosopher's Stone* or the union of opposing forces.

27.4 Transmutation of Emotions and States of Being

Alchemy seeks to transmute base substances into higher forms, and music has the ability to transmute emotions and states of being. Renaissance composers aimed to elicit emotional responses and provoke inner transformation through their compositions.

By combining specific melodic lines, harmonies, rhythms, and timbres, composers sought to guide listeners through a musical journey of emotional and spiritual growth. They aimed to create music that could transport the listener to different emotional and psychological states, ultimately leading to a sense of catharsis and transcendence.

27.5 Musical Temporalities and Cyclical Structures

Alchemy recognizes the cyclical nature of transformation, and music, with its temporal dimension, reflects this concept. Renaissance compositions often embraced cyclical structures, such as canons, fugues, and variations, mirroring the alchemical cycles of dissolution, transformation, and regeneration.

These cyclical musical forms represented the perpetual nature of alchemical processes and the eternal quest for higher states of being. They invited listeners to experience the transformative journey through repeated patterns, variations, and developments.

27.6 Musical Harmony and Divine Proportions

Alchemy seeks to understand the underlying harmonies of the universe, and music has long been associated with divine proportions and mathematical relationships. Renaissance composers, impelled by alchemical principles, explored the concept of musical harmony as a reflection of cosmic order and perfection.

Through the use of mathematical ratios, such as the golden ratio or the Fibonacci sequence, composers sought to create harmonically balanced compositions that resonated with the inherent order of the universe. These compositions were seen as embodying the divine harmonies and the alchemical pursuit of higher truths.

27.7 The Legacy of Alchemy in Music

The influence of alchemy in Renaissance music extends beyond the period itself, impacting subsequent musical traditions. The principles of harmony, balance, and symbolic expression continue to inform musical composition and performance to this day.

Contemporary composers and musicians draw upon alchemical concepts to create music that evokes transformation, inner journeying, and the exploration of the human psyche. The alchemical legacy in music serves as a reminder of the power of harmonies to touch the depths of our being and catalyze profound transformations.

In conclusion, alchemy's influence on Renaissance music highlights the deep interconnections between the arts, sciences, and philosophical thought. The alchemical language of symbolism, the quest for balance and harmony, the transmutation of emotions, the cyclical structures, the divine proportions, and the enduring legacy of alchemical principles in music all reflect the transformative power of sound and the human desire to express the ineffable. Through their compositions, Renaissance musicians sought to embody the alchemical journey and create harmonies that resonate with the transformative potential of the human spirit.

XXVIII: ALCHEMICAL ARCHITECTURE: SYMBOLIC STRUCTURES AND SACRED GEOMETRY

Architecture, with its ability to shape physical space and evoke emotional responses, has long been intertwined with symbolism and metaphysical concepts. In the realm of alchemy, architecture serves as a canvas for the embodiment of alchemical principles and the expression of profound symbolic meanings. In this chapter, we explore the world of alchemical architecture, focusing on its use of symbolic structures and *sacred geometry*.

28.1 Architecture as Alchemical Expression

Alchemy seeks to transform and transmute substances, while architecture, as an alchemical art form, aims to transform physical spaces into symbolic representations of higher truths. Alchemical architecture incorporates principles of *sacred geometry*, symbolic motifs, and intentional design to create spaces that facilitate spiritual and psychological transformation.

28.2 Sacred Geometry: Blueprint of the Universe

Sacred geometry, the study of geometric patterns and proportions found in nature, serves as the foundation of alchemical architecture. It is believed to reflect the underlying order and harmony of the universe. Architects use sacred geometric ratios, such as the golden ratio or the Fibonacci sequence, to create harmonious and aesthetically pleasing spaces that resonate with the divine order.

28.3 The Alchemical Temple

The temple, whether religious or esoteric, represents a physical manifestation of the alchemical journey. It serves as a sacred space where transformation and spiritual evolution can take place. The design and layout of the temple are carefully crafted to align with alchemical principles, employing symbolic elements and *sacred geometry* to create an environment conducive to inner exploration and communion with the divine.

28.4 The Labyrinth: Journey of the Soul

The *labyrinth* is a powerful alchemical symbol found in architectural design. It represents the journey of the soul, with its twists and turns, leading the seeker through various stages of transformation. Walking the *labyrinth* becomes a meditative experience, inviting introspection, self-reflection, and the integration of opposing forces.

28.5 Towers and Spires: Ascent to the Divine

Towers and spires, reaching toward the heavens, symbolize the ascent of consciousness and the connection between the earthly and the divine realms. They represent the alchemical quest for higher states of being and spiritual enlightenment. The verticality of these structures invokes a sense of transcendence and the aspiration to reach beyond the physical realm.

28.6 The Circle and the Mandala

The *circle*, a symbol of wholeness and unity, finds expression in alchemical architecture through the use of circular structures, such as domes or rotundas. These forms create a sense of harmony and balance, inviting individuals to experience a deeper connection with themselves and the surrounding space.

The *mandala*, a sacred geometric design representing the universe and the self, is often incorporated into alchemical architecture. *Mandalas* serve as focal points for meditation and contemplation, facilitating inner transformation and the integration of opposing forces.

28.7 Elemental Architecture

Alchemy recognizes the importance of the *four elements—earth, air, fire,* and *water*—in the alchemical processes. Alchemical architecture incorporates these elements, either symbolically or through the use of materials and design, to create spaces that evoke specific qualities and energies. For example, the use of natural materials like stone or wood connects the architecture to the element of *earth,* while open spaces or windows bring in the qualities of *air* and light.

28.8 The Alchemical Garden

The *alchemical garden* represents a harmonious blend of nature and human intervention. It incorporates alchemical principles into the design, layout, and selection of plants and materials. The garden serves as a metaphorical representation of the alchemical processes, with plants symbolizing the stages of growth, transformation, and the cycles of life.

28.9 Temporal and Ethereal Architecture

Alchemy recognizes the temporal nature of existence and the impermanence of physical structures. Temporary or ephemeral architecture, such as pavilions or installations, allows for the exploration of the transient nature of the alchemical journey. These structures may incorporate light, sound, and interactive elements to create immersive experiences that evoke the ephemeral and ethereal aspects of transformation.

28.10 The Alchemical Legacy in Contemporary Architecture

The legacy of alchemical architecture extends beyond the Renaissance period, influencing contemporary architectural design. Architects continue to incorporate alchemical principles, *sacred geometry*, and symbolic elements into their creations, seeking to create spaces that foster transformation, evoke spiritual contemplation, and reflect the interconnectedness of all things.

In conclusion, alchemical architecture serves as a vessel for the embodiment of alchemical principles and the expression of profound symbolic meanings. Through the use of *sacred geometry*, symbolic structures, and intentional design, alchemical architecture creates spaces that facilitate spiritual and psychological transformation. It invites individuals to embark on their own alchemical journey, exploring the depths of the self, and connecting with the universal principles of harmony and unity.

XXIX: ALCHEMICAL RECIPES AND EXPERIMENTS: UNVEILING THE LABORATORY SECRETS

The alchemical laboratory, with its array of apparatus and mysterious processes, served as the physical space for alchemists to conduct their experiments and seek the transmutation of substances. Within the laboratory, alchemical recipes and experiments were meticulously recorded, providing a roadmap for future practitioners. In this chapter, we dive into the world of alchemical recipes and experiments, unveiling some of the laboratory secrets of the alchemists.

29.1 The Language of Symbolism and Obscurity

Alchemical recipes and texts were often written in a language that blended symbolism, metaphor, and obscurity. This deliberate choice served multiple purposes. Firstly, it acted as a form of secrecy, protecting the valuable knowledge from those who were not initiated into the alchemical arts. Secondly, it reflected the belief that the true meaning of the recipes could only be understood by those who had undergone the inner alchemical journey.

29.2 The Importance of *Prima Materia*

Prima materia, meaning "first matter" or "raw material," was a crucial element in alchemical recipes and experiments. It referred to the base substance from which transformation was sought. Alchemists utilized various materials, including metals, minerals, and plants, as their *prima materia*. The choice of *prima materia* was influenced by symbolic associations, elemental qualities, and the desired outcome of the alchemical process.

29.3 The Process of Separation and Purification

One of the fundamental steps in alchemical experiments was the process of separation and purification. Alchemists sought to isolate and purify the desired components of their *prima materia*. Through techniques such as distillation, sublimation, and filtration, impurities were removed, allowing the essence of the substance to emerge.

29.4 Transmutation and the Philosopher's Stone

The ultimate goal of alchemical experiments was transmutation, the transformation of base substances into higher, more refined forms. The *Philosopher's Stone,* an elusive substance believed to possess powerful properties, was sought after as the key to achieving transmutation. Alchemical recipes and experiments often revolved around the quest for the *Philosopher's Stone,* offering instructions and insights into the process.

29.5 Laboratory Apparatus and Techniques

Alchemical laboratories were equipped with a variety of specialized apparatus and tools to facilitate the experiments. Distillation apparatus, alembics, retorts, and furnaces were among the essential equipment used for heating, cooling, and separating substances. Alchemists employed techniques such as calcination, fermentation, and coagulation to manipulate and transform their materials.

29.6 The Role of Observations and Documentation

Observation and documentation were crucial aspects of alchemical experiments. Alchemists meticulously recorded their observations, noting changes in color, texture, smell, and other physical properties. These detailed records served as a valuable reference for future experiments and contributed to the development of alchemical knowledge and understanding.

29.7 The Influence of Astrology and Planetary Hours

Astrology played a significant role in alchemical recipes and experiments. Alchemists believed that celestial influences affected the outcomes of their work. They aligned their experiments with specific astrological configurations and timed their processes according to the planetary hours. These astrological considerations were believed to enhance the efficacy of the alchemical operations.

29.8 Alchemical Recipes and the Oral Tradition

Alchemical recipes were often passed down through generations as part of an oral tradition. Master alchemists shared their knowledge and techniques with their apprentices, ensuring the preservation and continuity of the alchemical arts. This oral transmission contributed to the secrecy surrounding alchemical recipes and added to the aura of mystique surrounding the laboratory practices.

29.9 Alchemy and Herbalism

Alchemy and herbalism were closely intertwined, with alchemists recognizing the transformative properties of plants. Many alchemical recipes incorporated botanical ingredients, such as herbs, roots, and flowers. These plants were chosen for their symbolic associations, medicinal properties, and the potential to extract essential essences for the alchemical process.

29.10 The Legacy of Alchemical Recipes and Experiments

While alchemy's quest for transmutation of base substances into gold may not have been realized in a literal sense, the alchemical recipes and experiments left behind a rich legacy. They contributed to the development of chemistry, pharmaceuticals, and the understanding of materials. The systematic and meticulous approach of alchemists in recording their experiments paved the way for the scientific method and laid the groundwork for future advancements in the sciences.

In conclusion, alchemical recipes and experiments unveil the laboratory secrets of the alchemists, providing insights into their quest for transformation and transmutation. The language of symbolism and obscurity, the importance of *prima materia,* the process of separation and purification, the pursuit of the *Philosopher's Stone,* the use of specialized laboratory apparatus, the influence of astrology, and the legacy of alchemical recipes all contribute to the grand atlas of alchemical knowledge. These recipes and experiments serve as a testament to the alchemists' dedication, ingenuity, and the enduring quest for wisdom and transformation.

XXX: THE ENDURING MYSTERY OF ALCHEMY: UNANSWERED QUESTIONS AND SPECULATIONS

Alchemy, with its enigmatic symbolism and elusive goals, steadfastly engages the imagination and incites intrigue. Despite centuries of study and exploration, many aspects of alchemy remain shrouded in mystery, leaving unanswered questions and room for speculation. In this final chapter, we dive into the enduring mysteries of alchemy, contemplating the unresolved aspects that continue to fascinate scholars and enthusiasts.

30.1 The True Origins of Alchemy

One of the persistent mysteries surrounding alchemy is its true origins. While alchemical practices emerged in various civilizations throughout history, including ancient Egypt, Greece, and China, the precise origin point remains elusive. Some believe that alchemy originated in a single culture and spread to others, while others argue that it independently arose in different regions as a response to universal human yearnings for transformation and understanding.

30.2 The Alchemical Language and Symbolism

The language of alchemy, steeped in symbolism and obscurity, presents an ongoing challenge for interpretation. Despite extensive scholarship, there are still many symbols and allegorical texts that have not been fully deciphered. Some speculate that there may be deeper layers of meaning or hidden codes within alchemical texts, waiting to be unraveled by future generations.

30.3 The Philosopher's Stone: Myth or Reality?

The quest for the *Philosopher's Stone,* the legendary substance believed to possess transformative powers, remains an enduring mystery. While many alchemists pursued the *Philosopher's Stone,* its existence and properties continue to be subjects of speculation. Some view the *Philosopher's Stone* as a metaphorical symbol of spiritual enlightenment, while others believe that it may have had practical applications in ancient alchemical processes that have been lost to time.

30.4 The Connection Between Alchemy and Spiritual Traditions

Alchemy shares common themes and symbolism with various spiritual and mystical traditions, such as Hermeticism, Gnosticism, and Kabbalah. The precise nature of these connections and the influence of one upon the other is an ongoing area of exploration. Scholars and researchers continue to investigate the interplay between alchemical ideas and the spiritual philosophies of different cultures.

30.5 The Alchemical Elixir of Life

The pursuit of the alchemical elixir of life, a substance believed to grant immortality or prolonged vitality, has fascinated alchemists throughout history. Despite the countless experiments and explorations, the elixir of life has remained elusive.

Speculations abound regarding its composition, with some considering it a metaphorical representation of spiritual enlightenment or inner alchemical transformation.

30.6 The Practical Applications of Alchemical Knowledge

While alchemy is often associated with the transmutation of metals and the search for wealth, the practical applications of alchemical knowledge beyond metaphor and symbolism are still debated. Some speculate that alchemists may have made significant contributions to the development of early pharmaceuticals, chemical processes, and metallurgy, laying the groundwork for advancements in these fields.

30.7 The Influence of Alchemy on Art and Literature

Alchemy's impact on art and literature is undeniable, with countless works incorporating alchemical symbolism and themes. However, the precise extent of alchemy's influence and the intentions behind its integration into artistic and literary works are subjects of speculation. Some suggest that alchemical symbolism may have been used as a form of social commentary or as a means of expressing spiritual or philosophical ideas.

30.8 The Legacy of Alchemy in Modern Times

The legacy of alchemy continues to resonate in modern times, inspiring researchers, artists, and spiritual seekers. The enduring fascination with alchemy raises questions about its relevance today and its potential for guiding humanity towards deeper understandings of transformation, consciousness, and the mysteries of existence. Speculation abounds regarding the untapped wisdom that alchemy may still hold for our contemporary world.

30.9 The Unanswered Questions: Mysteries That Endure

As we conclude our exploration of alchemy, it is important to acknowledge that there are countless unanswered questions that continue to intrigue and challenge us. Alchemy's rich atlas of symbolism, its unresolved origins, the enigmatic language of its texts, the elusive nature of the *Philosopher's Stone,* the connections with spiritual traditions, the practical applications of its knowledge, and its enduring legacy are all areas that invite further speculation and investigation.

In the face of these mysteries, we are reminded of the alchemical journey itself—an ongoing process of exploration, transformation, and discovery. The quest for knowledge and understanding propels us forward, drawing us deeper into the fascinating realm of alchemy.

In conclusion, the enduring mystery of alchemy invites speculation and contemplation. While some questions may never be fully answered, the pursuit of knowledge and the exploration of the alchemical arts are still with us to illuminate new insights and initiate further inquiry. Alchemy's enduring legacy lies in its ability to expand our imaginations, challenge our understanding of the world, and encourage us to seek the hidden truths that lie within ourselves and the universe.

Ω

OMEGA

Dear reader of the Esoteric Religious Studies Series, we express our deepest gratitude for embarking on this enlightening journey. Having dived into the realms of esoteric wisdom, may you carry the flame of knowledge within your being. May the insights gained and the revelations experienced guide your path as you traverse the atlas of life. May the wisdom you have acquired permeate every aspect of your existence, nurturing your spirit and inspiring your actions. May you continue to seek truth, embrace growth, and walk the path of wisdom with grace and compassion. May your life be a testament to the transformative power of esoteric knowledge.

If you have enjoyed the words of this book, please consider leaving a review in the marketplace you found it so that its content can enrich the lives of others.

Other Books in This Series

1. Hermeticism and Alchemy in Renaissance Europe
2. Gnosticism: Ancient Mystical Traditions, Sects & Texts
3. Zoroastrianism: Esoteric Teachings and the Priesthood of the Fire
4. Sufism: Persian Mystical Path of Islam
5. Daoist Immortality and Internal Alchemy
6. Theurgy and Neoplatonic Mysticism
7. Shamanism in Siberia: Animism and Nature Worship
8. African Traditional Religions and Spirituality
9. Druidism and Celtic Mysticism
10. Indigenous Australian Dreamtime, Songlines and Ancestral Beings
11. Jyotish: Vedic Astrology
12. Hellenistic Mystery Cults: Thessalian Witchcraft & Ancient Greek Magic
13. Kabbalah: Jewish Mystical Tradition
14. Shinto: Japanese Indigenous Religion
15. Native American Spirituality and Vision Quests
16. Mesoamerican Shamanism and Divination
17. Ancient Egyptian Rituals and Symbolism
18. Norse Mythology and Runes
19. Rastafarianism: Spirituality and Social Movement
20. Jainism: Ascetic Practices and Philosophy
21. Romuva: Baltic Paganism, Witchcraft, and Folklore Revival
22. Vodou: Haitian Creole Religion
23. Maori Spirituality and Creation Myths
24. Hawaiian Huna Healing and Spirituality
25. Theosophy: Blending Eastern and Western Esotericism
26. Tibetan Bon: Ancient Shamanistic Tradition
27. Yoruba Religion and Orisha Worship
28. Esoteric Buddhism: Secret Teachings and Rituals
29. Romani Folklore and Mythology
30. Aztec Mythology and Cosmology
31. Bahá'í Faith: Unity of Religions
32. Hittite Religion and Rituals
33. Spiritualism: Communication with the Spirit World
34. Afro-Caribbean Syncretic Religions
35. Tantra: Ritual Practices and Symbolism
36. Armenian Folk Religion and Beliefs
37. Guarani Mythology and Cosmology
38. Esoteric Aspects of Islam: Batiniyya and Hurufism
39. Manichaeism: Dualistic Religion and Philosophy
40. Finnish Shamanism and Folk Magic
41. Ancient Sumerian Religion and Magic
42. Afro-Brazilian Umbanda and Candomblé
43. Tibetan Oracles and Divination Practices
44. Khoisan Spirituality: San Bushmen Traditions
45. Yezidi Religion: Angel Worship and the Sacred Peacock
46. Kalash Religion: Ancient Indo-Aryan Practices
47. Druze Esotericism: Secret Wisdom and Reincarnation
48. Burmese Nat Worship and Spirit Possession
49. Ancient Canaanite Religion: Rituals, Magical Texts and Spells
50. Etruscan Divination and Augury

51. Ainu Shamanism: Spiritual Practices in Northern Japan
52. Circassian Paganism and Ancestral Customs
53. Tengrism: Central Asian Shamanistic Beliefs
54. Mari El Paganism: Volga-Finnic Indigenous Religion
55. Haida Mythology and Totemism: Healing and Spirit Communication
56. Balinese Hindu-Buddhist Syncretism
57. Aramean Religion and Ancient Semitic Cults
58. Khoekhoen Religion: Southern African Indigenous Beliefs
59. Ojibwe Midewiwin: The Grand Medicine Society
60. Afro-Colombian Religions: Palenque and Santeria
61. Sámi Shamanism: Indigenous Spirituality of Northern Europe
62. Ossetian Folk Religion and Mythology
63. Mithraism: Ancient Mystery Cult of the Roman Empire
64. Ainu Bear Festival and Symbolism
65. Ancient Anatolia: Hittites and Luwians, and Lydian Goddess Cults
66. Toda Shamanism: Indigenous People of South India
67. Mesopotamian Magic and Incantations
68. Mande Paganism: West African Traditional Religions
69. Javanese Kejawen: Mystical Teachings and Rituals
70. Thracian Myth and Greco-Roman Orphic and Dionysian Mysteries
71. Maronite Christianity: Esoteric Practices and Traditions
72. Basque Mythology, Folklore, and Witchcraft
73. Gagauz Folk Religion and Rituals
74. Tagalog Mythology: Anito Spirits and Mythical Creatures
75. Hurrian Religion: Ancient Near Eastern Pantheon
76. Buryat Buddhism: Shamanistic Elements in Tibetan Buddhism
77. Selk'nam Cosmology and Ceremonies
78. Baka Pygmy Spirituality: Central African Indigenous Beliefs
79. Kumyk Paganism: Turkic Indigenous Religion
80. Scythian Religion and Warrior Culture
81. Venda Mythology: Sacred Lake and Rainmaker Rituals
82. Onondaga Longhouse Religion: Iroquois Spiritual Practices
83. Ewe-Fon Voodoo: West African Spiritual Practices
84. Manchu Shamanism: Indigenous Spirituality of Northeast Asia
85. Taíno Religion: Indigenous Beliefs of the Caribbean
86. Ancient Moabite Religion: Worship of Chemosh and Ashtaroth
87. Gallo-Roman Religion: Celtic Influence in Roman Gaul
88. Tsimshian Mythology: Stories of Raven and Trickster Figures
89. Manobo Indigenous Spirituality: Mindanao Tribal Beliefs
90. Pawnee Sacred Bundles and Tribal Ceremonies
91. Batak Shamanism: Indigenous Practices of North Sumatra
92. Breton Folklore: Legends and Supernatural Beings
93. Jivaroan Shamanism: Indigenous Traditions of the Amazon Rainforest
94. Alawite Mystical Teachings and Secret Practices
95. Silesian Folk Religion and Folklore
96. Igbo Odinani: Traditional Religion of the Igbo People
97. Rarámuri Shamanism: Indigenous Spirituality of the Tarahumara
98. Kikuyu Traditional Religion: Sacred Sites and Ancestor Worship
99. Ancient Numidian Religion: North African Indigenous Beliefs
100. Lurs Folk Religion and Rituals

A WORLD OF ESOTERIC THOUGHT

Printed in Great Britain
by Amazon

33431335R00139